Throughout this elegant book McPhee never loses his focus or his purpose—to cut through all the techno-babble, the airs and poses, the intimidating vocabulary, all the impediments that would come between man and the joyously simple act of moving by wind and water. This book is pure invitation to the world of sail.

–Tony Chamberlain,
Sailing Editor of *The Boston Globe*

CYCLING
by Arlene Plevin
HIKING
by Cindy Ross
RUNNING
by John Schubert

Forthcoming

CLIMBING

CROSS-COUNTRY SKIING

SCUBA DIVING

SKIING

SAILING

A CELEBRATION OF THE SPORT AND THE WORLD'S BEST PLACES TO ENJOY IT

———

by MICHAEL B. McPHEE

Illustrations by Peg Magovern

Travel section by Lisa Gosselin

———

A RICHARD BALLANTINE/BYRON PREISS BOOK

Sailing: A Celebration of the Sport and the World's Best Places to Enjoy It

Series Editor: Richard Ballantine
Design Director: Byron Preiss
Editor: Babette Lefrak
Associate Editor: Brendan Healey
Contributor: Peter Oliver
Designers: Stephen Brenninkmeyer and Wendy Helft
Illustrator: Peg Magovern
Cover Design: Fabrizio La Rocca
Cover Photograph: David Brownell/The Image Bank
Cover Illustrator: Marco Marinucci

Special thanks to Kristina Peterson, Publisher of Fodor's; Michael Spring, Editorial Director of Fodor's; Nin Chi, Kathy Huck, Nellie Kurtzman, Rosana Ragusa, Jessica Steinberg, also Boat US, the U.S. Coast Guard, the American Red Cross, Cruising World/Sailing World magazine, Motor Boating & Sailing *magazine,* Sail *magazine,* Yachting *magazine.*

Illustrations on pps. 32, 33, 34, 55, 58 & 73 by Nin Chi, on pps. 149-151 courtesy of *Sailing World* magazine, on pps. 33 & 35 courtesy of the U.S. Coast Guard, on page 53 courtesy of Hunter Marine Corporation

To Barbara Lloyd, a true and gracious friend; and to John Guare, my greatest influence who constantly shows me there is no ceiling to life. Love and thanks to both. And for my mother, Ursula, whom I never got to know.

CONTENTS

Acknowledgments

A book involves so much more than writing. Many thanks to Richard Ballantine, a truly gifted editor who took my storm-tossed prose and turned it into spinnaker reading. We started this project on the Marblehead waterfront and finished on top of Mt. Tamalpais. May we do it 100 times more. Thanks to Brendan Healey, who patiently fielded all my rantings and ravings and turned them into something positive.

I want to thank my great friends Barb and Paul Benoit of Newburyport, Massachusetts; Ann and Walter Nickerson of Newport, Rhode Island; and Mary Lou and Ernie Schnorf of Lagunitas, California; who not only opened their homes and refrigerators to me but their hearts as well. Everyone should be blessed with friends like them.

Thanks to Lou and Amy Calvert for their love and support and to Jim Schermerhorn for his belief in me. Get your novel published! Thanks to George and Jenny Hill, Gisela Huffman, "Dad" Hollamby, Lynn Santer, Boo and Bob Metzger, Chaz Moore, and to Ted Davis who generously took me sailing again on *Vaga*, which he has beautifully restored.

Thanks also to my father, Robbie, and my stepmother, Mary.

SAILING

INTRODUCTION

There is nothing, absolutely nothing, half so much worth doing as messin' about in boats, in 'em or out of 'em, doesn't matter.

> —Water Rat in *The Wind in the Willows*

Sailing is wonderfully democratic. You do not need to have exceptional strength, ironman endurance, or extraordinary wealth to enjoy sailing, even to become quite good at it. In fact, sailing is one of the few sports you get better at as you become older.

To be a good sailor, though, you must enjoy the beauty of the water, land, and air, and living and working with these natural elements. Weather is often unpredictable, but to a sailor, weather is a challenge rather than a threat.

To be a good sailor, you must be competent at boat handling and basic navigation. You must be able to make machinery work, to anticipate breakdowns and failures, and when necessary, fix them. You must be able to think and plan ahead, and appreciate order and efficiency, yet not be overwhelmed by the unexpected.

Good sailors are "doers" who find intrinsic enjoyment in challenges, and in work well done. The core of sailing is living with nature and the elements—maintaining boats so that they are lovely and seaworthy, and continuously learning and honing the skills to sail them in all conditions.

Sailing is unique among sports because it can be enjoyed in so many ways and at so many levels. Some sailors stick to little skiffs on lakes and bays. Others like to charter boats with professional crews. Some sailors like to spend weekends on their boats, others like to voyage to distant ports. Many like to race, so much so that any two boats sailing in the same direction automatically compete.

Whether you are young or old, whether you gracefully glide in a small day sailer or boom along in a massive 150-foot schooner, sailing touches you inside.

In *Forgiving Wind, On Becoming a Sailor* Fred Pawledge writes:

> . . . I love sailing because it gives me things that make me feel good: things that are worthy and lasting and that both stretch my brain and please my eye; that demand from me the skills that I have learned; that reward me for doing the right things; that (more often than not, at least) are forgiving in their punishment when I do something wrong. Paradoxically—for sailing really must be done according to a large number of rules and constraints—sailing gives me a great deal of freedom.
>
> Finally, when things are going well and even some times when they aren't, sailing gives me a reminder of the immortality that we all used to think we had, back when we were kids. When you learn to sail, you learn a good deal about yourself. And you become a little more free.

Joseph Conrad, perhaps the greatest writer to sail, wrote of the symbiosis between men and ships: "To deal with men is as fine an art as it is to deal with ships. Both men and ships live in an unstable element, are subject to subtle and powerful influences, and want to have their merits understood rather than their faults found out."

"The sea calls us to action," wrote American William Albert Robinson, the first person to circumnavigate the world with a two-man crew, in the early 1930s. "I am in my element when the breakers come foaming over my bow and my wake is aboil behind me."

—*Michael B. McPhee*

BEGINNINGS

Growing up far from the ocean, in Aspen, Colorado, I never gave much thought to sailing. If you don't see sailboats, you don't think about them. Once when I went rummaging through Dad's navy stuff, I found a small handbook on the ABC's of sailing, which I flipped through but did not understand. No one I knew had a boat, other than canoes and kayaks. I used to kayak a fair amount, and take inner tubes down the white water rivers. But big, open water was simply not part of my childhood, and I was 18 the first time I swam in the ocean.

In the summer after my sophomore year in college, I moved back up to Aspen. I had a beautiful place to housesit, an old jeep, a couple of lawnmowers, and a bike. Mornings consisted of riding my bike a few miles up Independence Valley to some fishing holes on the Roaring Fork River. There was a half-hour window shortly after sunrise when the trout would feed; if I got situated in time, I always caught three or four good ones—together with wild asparagus from the parks and watercress from the river, my dinner. Days consisted of mowing lawns and landscaping, which I enjoyed immensely. In the evenings, I would play tennis or take a hike, then head into town at night for friends and music. Life was good, and simple. I had no great needs or wants, until. . . .

Driving down Main Street one day, I saw a fantasy come to life. This great looking woman in cut-off shorts stepped off the curb, looked right at me and stuck her thumb out. She was tall, with an athlete's build, and had long, dirty-blonde hair and freckles. I screeched to a stop.

As she jumped in, we both laughed at the sea of Coke cans, pizza boxes, and other trash in the jeep. She said she had one just like it back home in Westhampton.

"Oh, so you're from California," I said with my worldly knowledge.

"No, New York. You know. Long Island," she said.

I thought Long Island was a parking lot for New York City.

This was one of those chance meetings that go right, in spite of the nerdy things I said. Her name was Hillary, and she was in Aspen for the summer, trying the mountains for the first time. I couldn't think of a better person to show her the mountains than me. So off we went, and my life took an enormous turn. We spent a lot of time together during that following winter. Hillary loved the mountains, but never really got comfortable living in them. She missed the ocean, a yearning which I learned was common for most people who grew up near the sea. On the other hand, most of us who grew up in the mountains can move down to the sea and feel fine.

Hillary used to talk a lot about sailing and boats and fishing and the beach, and the following summer she invited me home to meet her parents and to spend the month of August by the sea.

My image of Long Island had always been of buildings and pavement, and maybe one tree. I had no idea the island was more than 100 miles long, or that the eastern end was gorgeous, with truck farms, bays and clam flats, or that I would instantly like it. I liked all the winding bays and estuaries, the architecture, the big shade trees and the smell of the ocean. And I liked all the funny names, like Shinnecock and Quoque and Montauk.

Hillary's family lived in a beautiful stone house, not large but solid, with a circular driveway in the back, separating a large barn and guest house from the main residence. The house was musty, in a good sense like so many old dwellings near the water. Inside it had lots of wood molding and lots of brass—clocks and barometers and stuff. The dark bookcases in the den were laden with heavy books on sailing, boat design, and sail trim.

The next morning, with dew on the grass and a thick, muggy haze in the air, Hillary took me down a dirt path toward the water. On the left were some old poultry sheds with rusty hinges, and on the right was a split-rail fence enclosing Eeyore, their donkey. We walked another 50 yards down the path under a canopy of large oak and maple trees. As we reached the end of the path, I gasped as I looked out over a beautiful blue bay extending way out to some white sand dunes you could barely see. To the left were expansive green lawns coming down to gazebos and docks. To the right were big estates with white houses and black shutters, tennis courts, and even a helicopter pad. What a spot.

In front of us was a wooden dock, which we walked out on. Not more than 20 feet out in the water was Hillary's little sailboat. I can't recall seeing anything prettier. It just sat there on the glassy water, floating so gracefully. A tiny breeze turned it on its mooring, so we could see it sideways. Almost humanlike, it was showing off, knowing full well that we would approve.

The comparison between Hillary and her boat was immediate. The sloop had the most graceful lines, lean and strong, with nothing extra that would give bulk or heaviness. It was made of Honduras mahogany, brightly varnished and deep tan in color. The sails were crispy white. It had an elegance to it, and moved easily and effortlessly.

We rowed a skiff out to the little boat. Hillary, in her white summer dress, stepped into the sloop and offered me her hand. We raised the sails, the sloop heeled, and we glided away. I swooned. What a wonderful day. I knew from that moment on that some part of me would always be involved with sailboats.

Hillary and I sailed every day. We would sail across the bay and go swimming in the ocean. We would sail down to other villages, or to friends' houses, or just around the bay. It was real Huck Finn stuff.

Hillary also introduced me to another side of sailing. Her father, Ansell, owned the *Rahnee*, built in 1890 and the oldest registered yacht in the country. *Rahnee* was a man's boat with heavy framing, stout gaff-rigged spars and massive fittings. The sails were huge and heavy, requiring cooperation among the skipper, the crew and the wind. Once in position, the sails could be tightened only by thick lines wrapped around bronze winches cranked with long handles. I liked Ansell a lot, and respected his knowledge of boats and the sea. In a sense, he too was like his boat— very traditional, both handsome without any fluff, and pretty much no-nonsense.

Visiting with Hillary's family was wonderful. We went body surfing, skinny dipping, digging for clams, even

crewing on a commercial fishing dragger one day, and—
the best of all seashore traditions—we ate at an old-fashioned clambake one night.

There is no finer way of eating than to dig a big pit in
the beach, build a fire under some large rocks, then fill
the entire pit with wet seaweed, lobsters, clams, mussels,
corn, potatoes, sausage, and anything else. Cover it with a
tarp and let it steam for three or four hours. A plate of
that with a cold glass of beer on a warm summer night at
the beach is finer than any feast I've been to, including
any pig roast or barbecue.

All in all, it was a great trip, and I was sad to leave—
especially without Hillary, who stayed to go to college at
Cornell.

After I got back to Colorado, I went over to the
house of my best friends, Jimmy Cassell and his wife
Debbi. All I wanted to talk about was sailing, and the
whole new world out there floating before the wind.
Jimmy, a musician and an electrical engineer with an
insatiable curiosity, was intrigued by the problem of moving a sailboat against the wind. I gave a half-baked expla-
nation involving something about airplane wings and lift
off a curved section. A friend of Jimmy's, Chris Calahan,
who had joined us for dinner, smiled a Cheshire cat smile
as I fumbled with explanations about ballast, halyards, and
tacks. Then he casually asked if we would like to take a
sail—right here in Colorado! A friend of his had a Hobie
Cat and was always looking for people to join him sailing
on the local reservoir.

He had to ask just once for us to be at his house early Saturday morning, ready to do anything to experience this new-found form of confusion. At the reservoir, Jimmy and I climbed on board and took the ride of our lives. Hillary's sloop had been designed for lazing around small bays and lakes. Hobie Cats were designed by a California surfer, Hobie Alter, to do one thing—go as fast as possible across the water, even over waves, without an engine. If Hillary's sloop was a nice old Mercedes convertible with leather seats, this Hobie Cat was a Harley Sportster. Fast as hell and not very comfortable. You just sat where you could hang on, keep your head up and be ready to move.

The three of us rocketed back and forth across the reservoir several times until Chris finally found a good puff of wind and lifted one of the pontoons out of the water. There we were, several feet up in the air, trying not to slide down a 30-degree nylon trampoline, while the lower pontoon knifed through the green water at 12 or 13 miles an hour, a frightfully fast speed for a sailboat.

Lifting the hull out terrified us, but in a way that we wanted more. The wind died, the airborne hull splashed into the water and Chris masterfully spun the the boat 45 degrees toward the beach.

"She-e-e-e-e-yit," Jimmy and I yelled at each other. Not another word was needed. We had to get one of these things. No question about it.

Through that winter, we kept one eye on the want ads for Hobie Cats. In mid-March we found a used one, in very good shape, for about $1,700. We had been stripping old, weathered barns of their siding and selling it as

interior paneling, making a very good profit; over the winter, we'd paid for our tuition, books, Cassell's first kid, Damon, and still had enough cash for the boat.

In mid-April, we took our Hobie out to Cherry Creek Reservoir just outside of Denver. The ice had melted just two weeks before and that was good enough for us. In the parking lot we set up the mast and rigging, normally about a 10-minute job. Without instructions, and only a vague memory from last summer of what a Hobie should look like, an hour had passed before we had the boat assembled.

Luckily, we were sensible enough to wear life jackets. For we had barely climbed aboard and shoved it off the beach when we hit a gust of wind and flipped over. The owner who had sold the Hobie to us had practiced how to right the boat with us, so we didn't take too long getting it back up. But no sooner did we right it than another gust hit us and pushed us over again. This time we "turtled" or went over 180 degrees. We were still so close to shore that the mast stuck in the soft mud on the bottom of the reservoir.

Three of us sat and pulled on one hull, and with considerable effort we brought the boat back up and scrambled on board, out of the freezing 48 degree water. By now, we were trying to catch our breath and collect our thoughts. We were still laughing, but we were getting nervous. As pretender to the helmsman, I knew probably better than anyone that we were on the verge of trouble. We hadn't even started to control the boat. We couldn't choose a direction and sail; we couldn't even keep the boat upright. If it had been in July, with warm water and plenty of other boats around, it would have been fine. But now we were cold and there were only two other boats out, both fishing.

With the sails flapping and all the lines loose, we tried to figure out what we needed to do to stay upright. We hadn't even thought of getting to shore yet, all we cared about was keeping the damn thing upright! Finally, we felt sure enough to trim the sails in, maneuver the rudder somewhat toward the shore, and hope for the best.

Luck was not with us. We couldn't get the thing pointed toward the shore. The faster we sailed, the more confused we got, trying to bring it around—and then another gust hit us and knocked us over for the third time. Suddenly, we all knew it was serious—that sailing was over for the day and that we quickly had to get out of the freezing water.

One of the fishermen had seen us go over again and had the same feelings we did, that things were out of control. He motored over and threw us a line, which I tied to the downwind pontoon. His prop churned, the line went taut and gradually the Hobie turned upright.

I immediately pulled the sail down. Without spoken words, the fisherman nodded to pull us into shore. I was so cold that I started shivering violently. I was shaking so hard I couldn't keep my eyes focused on anything.

A disastrous start to sailing our own boat. But we were far from discouraged.

In typical fashion, that next week, I noticed a blurb in the paper about a Hobie Cat regatta in two weeks, every-one welcome. I called the number and some guy said to come along, the club members would be more than happy to show us how to sail and even how to race.

Deciding to learn as much as possible before then, with hopes of never looking so foolish again, I went down to the Denver Public Library and checked out three books on how to sail. Jimmy and I pored over them, even making little paper boats with sails. We used a fan to figure out what was going on, what a starboard tack was and how a boat went into irons. What the hell was buoy room?

We drove 100 miles to the regatta, up over an 11,000 foot pass that the snow plows had only recently opened. Hillary, if only you could see what you started. Now Jimmy and I were towing a sailboat through six-foot high corridors of snow, reading books to each other on how to sail.

On the beach at Grand Lake, we found a whole group of Hobie Cat sailors more than willing to show us how to rig the mast and to share in the story of our catastrophe on Cherry Creek Reservoir. Everyone had a similar story of near disasters and true buffoonery to share.

Throughout the years of sailing, I have learned one absolute rule—that whatever predicament you end up in, you're not the first one there, nor will you be the last. And the sailors I respect the most generally are the ones most willing to share their misfortunes as well as their knowledge.

With some support and a chance to learn what we were doing, the Hobie became more enjoyable. Everyone said to join in the regatta; it would be a great way to learn. So we walked across the road to the Grand Lake Yacht Club, unofficially the highest elevation yacht club in the world, and joined the regatta!

Mimicking the fleet, we raised our mainsail and tightened the lines exactly when everyone else did. When the others shoved off the beach for the start of the first race, we took a deep breath, and shoved off too.

The first race was completely uneventful. With very light winds, we steered clear of the congestion at the starting line. Steered clear is an understatement. We didn't cross the line until 10 minutes after the start. Not only that, we didn't finish until after the second race had already started. What did we care? We were sailing our own boat, and we were dry.

We eventually got the hang of the boat and decided we might be slightly more aggressive in the third race. In the confusion of jockeying for position at the start, though, we could not predict what anyone was going to do. Consequently, I came in too close behind one boat and drove one of my pontoons clear up onto it. Through the yelling and shouting, no one was hurt, only my pride. The skipper of the other boat merely shoved us off and faced forward to concentrate on his race.

By the end of that summer, Jimmy and I had made considerable progress. We sailed all the time, with family, friends, and even by ourselves. As a team, we worked our way up through the fleet, and once even had a shot at winning.

At a regatta at Dillon Reservoir, a hotshot blond couple from California showed up with a slick Hobie—obviously the boat to beat on that day. They easily won the morning race. In the afternoon race, to everyone's surprise, Jimmy and I rounded the last mark and headed for the finish line—in the lead. We had maneuvered past everyone, including the Californians. This was a shoo-in for our first win. All we had to do was sail a straight course. The breeze was strong, which favored us because both Jimmy and I were fairly heavy and able to keep the boat down.

Hobie Cats have a minimum weight requirement for the crew of 285 pounds. Most crews try to stay near that weight. Some medium-sized guys sail with their wives. One 270-pounder even sailed with his dog. Jimmy and I were stuck with each other, coming in at 388 pounds, which gave us an advantage in hurricanes.

So here we come around the last mark in first place, with a clear shot to the finish line in strong winds. Just hike out, hold the boat down, and steer straight. We set the sails, Jimmy climbed onto the rail to hike out, and, in his excitement, forgot to hook into his harness. He hiked out and fell right off the boat. The sonovabitch.

I knew I could hold that boat down myself and finish. I glanced at Jimmy, in 50-degree water, and he knew immediately what I was thinking. Against my will, I slacked the sails off, turned the boat around and picked him up. By now he was turning blue. California and three other boats whizzed past us as I dragged my water-logged partner from the water.

Jimmy and I persisted in racing, always looking to improve our performance, and by the end of the season we had won both a heavy-air race and a light-air race— undeniable proof that we were learning our lessons well.

For the next two summers, I sailed my Hobie Cat nearly every weekend, and on many evenings in between. My general confidence, and boat handling ability, grew a little bit each time. I felt good because I was becoming proficient at something totally foreign to me just a short while ago.

That gave me great pleasure, as did the sailing itself. It's one thing to go along for a ride on someone else's boat, another thing entirely to be the owner of the boat. You face a greater number of problems, questions, challenges, responsibilities. It's the difference between driving a car and being a passenger—the driver will have a far better recollection of the route.

Another thing I liked about sailing was that the greatest risk of trying something new was merely a dunking, and drenched pride. Short of a collision, it's hard to seriously injure yourself.

The pinnacle of sailing our Hobie Cat came when my roommate Wizzo and I trailered the Hobie out to San Francisco. From the deck of a boat on San Francisco Bay we looked out over one of the most glorious harbors in the world. San Francisco is a lovely city, a patchwork quilt of buildings and houses blanketing the hills. The Golden Gate Bridge, from the water, is awesome. Anywhere within sight of the bridge, the bay is rough sailing, usually with 20 to 25 knots of wind and fairly choppy water.

Out on the Hobie Cat, it was cold and rough and salty. It was all we could do to hold down the Hobie, and twice it was more than we could do. I felt like an explorer in a hostile environment. The adrenaline

pumped as we dashed out around Alcatraz, then sped to the threshold of open ocean, under the Golden Gate Bridge, Neptune tempting us to venture further out.

Yet, as soon as we sailed around behind one of the hills of Sausalito, or behind the city and out of the wind tunnel formed by the bridge, the boat calmed right down; we would warm up, dry off, and enjoy a most civilized cruise with both hulls in the water.

During my last year at the University of Colorado, the sailing fever really gripped me. Living in a cabin at 8,000 feet, I'd trudge through the snow to the mailbox looking for the latest issue of *Sail* magazine, wondering if any other subscribers lived so close to timberline.

Because of my summertime visits to the East Coast, I had made up my mind to start my newspaper career in New England. I had come across the eloquent writings of John Cole of the *Maine Times*, whose love of Maine and the ocean inspired me. Soon after graduating, in 1974, I sold my Hobie, packed up and drove to New England, to become a newspaperman and a sailor.

A two-week search for a job ended in the newsroom of *The Standard-Times* of New Bedford, Massachusetts: "Mike, we've got a job we think you'll like," said John Early, the kind, Archibald Cox-type managing editor. "It's covering the island of Nantucket."

Nantucket? An island. They're sending me out to an island? It sounded like the Siberia of journalism. I had an ominous feeling this was not the path to newspaper stardom. But I agreed to look over the island and come back in a few days with an answer.

The next day, I was in Hyannis, Massachusetts, on Cape

Cod, on the same sandy beaches trod by JFK, Eugene O'Neill, and so many other well-known East Coast names. I boarded the ferry and sat up front on the open bow, mesmerized by the steady heaving of the ship, the white, foaming bow wave and the endless crying of the seagulls, who followed us the entire 25 miles across to Nantucket.

The ferry entered the Nantucket channel, rounded the Brant Point lighthouse and came into Nantucket Harbor. The scene was picture-perfect: A quaint little town sloped gracefully down to the harbor, with two white church steeples in the background like silent sentries. Gray shingled buildings lined the waterfront, with people milling around the stores and marina. Sailboats rested at their moorings. Places like this exist only in movies, I thought.

Once ashore, I walked and walked and walked; out to the beach, down Main Street with its funny cobblestones that rattled the teeth right out of the bicyclists, down to the marina. There was too much to take in at once, but it felt good, and I was sure I had found the place of my dreams, to live and work in, and learn about the sea and sailing.

I moved to Nantucket in the fall of 1974. Rapidly, I began meeting people who couldn't have been warmer and friendlier. So much for the stereotype of cold, aloof New Englanders, especially islanders. Soon, I found a housesitting job in a beautiful old house built by a sea captain. And shortly after that, on the door of a shabby little office downtown I nailed up the sign: Nantucket Bureau Chief. A year later, *New York Times* columnist Russell Baker would joke to me that, despite his and his esteemed cohorts having been bureau chiefs in Moscow, Paris, and Washington, none of them had ever been

promoted to Nantucket Bureau Chief!

I found much to report about the town government, the schools, the police and fire departments—a crash course on the workings of a small New England town. But it was the island's relationship with the sea that fascinated me. Fishing for the bay scallops, from November to March, involved nearly half the population; the fishermen out every dawn somehow managing to stay warm; the scallop cutters who worked into the night in unheated shanties cutting open the sweet mollusks; the truckers, the buyers, the brokers and finally the bankers. I got right on their boats, and pulled the dredges with them. I even learned to cut scallops, and occasionally eat a few raw.

The offshore lobstermen had their own microcosm, and fleet. Some fished more than 100 miles out, on the edge of the Continental Shelf, for three days before returning with up to 1,500 pounds of the delicate crustacean. I accepted an invitation for one of those trips, which became my introduction to disabling seasickness. I spent three days leaning over the rail, losing all interest in the dolphins, the Russian fishing fleets, and anything resembling food. I even passed up the crew's traditional final meal of lobster before heading in.

That first winter, I found myself spending more and more time wandering through the island's boatyards, which were filled with yachts waiting for fresh coats of paint and varnish in time for next summer. Gradually, I got to know the carpenters, riggers, and sail-makers in the boatyards, and began to learn about yachts.

I decided it was time to buy a boat and experience the sea myself. It seemed only natural to look for a wooden

boat. After all, I was living in the land of Moby Dick—
of Nantucket sleigh rides, where men in rowboats once
harpooned whales, then tied the harpoon line to the
rowboat and held on for dear life until the whale tired
and died, and of 200-year-old sea captains' homes. It
seemed heretical to buy a fiberglass boat.

I did not know exactly what I was looking for, but I
wanted something around 25 feet long that could readily
go to sea, yet be easy to handle. I wanted a boat with a
bunk or two, and a stove on which I could make coffee.
It signified independence—being able to go out to sea
and have a cup of coffee while lying on my bunk.

After exhausting the inventory of sailboats on the
island, I began taking my car off-island, "to America," as
the islanders called it, to look for boats. I roamed all over
the Massachusetts coast—Padanaram, Marion, Mattapoisett, Hyannis. I started driving to Rhode Island and
clear into Connecticut. Then I went north, to Marblehead, Manchester, Newburyport, and finally Down East,
into Maine. I found lots of old wooden boats, the kind
I'd read about—Herreshoffs, Aldens, and Hinckleys—
beautiful boats classified by the name of their designers.

I started to see what these master architects had
designed and to appreciate the extraordinary abilities of
the craftsmen who fashioned the designs into living
boats—graceful, sleek yachts which were well founded
and strong, yet able to ride in the water with a lightness
and vitality which masked their strength.

In Boothbay Harbor in Maine, I climbed up onto a
snow-covered boat and knew right away my search was
over. It was a Folkboat, a lovely little 25-foot sloop with a

small cabin and two berths, a nice-sized cockpit and a tall mast. It was built with a lapstrake hull, where the planks overlap like clapboards rather than being butted smooth.

The Folkboat design was initiated by the king of Sweden, who, right after World War II, took Germany's idea for the Volkswagon, or "people's car," and applied it to a boat. He held a contest among boat designers to come up with a small, seaworthy boat that the masses could afford—a people's boat. The Folkboat was the winner and proved so popular that thousands were made. Many have found their way to the United States, either on board ships or sailed over by their owners. The largest fleet today is in San Francisco Bay.

After finding four Folkboats for sale, I settled on *Vaga* (Swedish for voyage), at a bargain price. *Vaga* was in good shape except for some broken ribs on the left side. A man I had recently made friends with, Armin Elsaesser, said he would be happy to help me fix them, and teach me at the same time.

An entire new world opened up to me, that of working on wooden boats. Throw away the square, the level, and the straightedge. Boat woodworking, I learned, was like nothing else. I also learned that sailboats, particularly wooden boats, require a lot of maintenance. Skill at repairs is an integral part of sailing. Most sailors cannot afford to have all of their maintenance done for them. More importantly, if something breaks while out sailing—usually the case—you've got to be able to do your own repairs. Being handy with tools is as important as knowing where the wind is coming from. And, for many

Costs

How much does it cost? "If you have to ask, you can't afford it," is the much-quoted reply by J.P. Morgan. But that's not true today. Sailboats can be relatively inexpensive.

If you're just starting out, there's absolutely no reason not to buy a used boat—for example, a Laser, Sunfish, Dragon, or Lightning. These range from as little as $1,000 all the way up to $10,000. Make sure you get a good trailer. Good, used Hobie Cats are well worth it, and can be found for as little as $750 with trailer. Plan on $200 to $300 a year for maintenance.

Cruisers can begin around $4,000 or $5,000 and run up well into six figures. Maintenance, including moorings, yard bills, storage, and launching, can cost $2,000 a year and up.

A good, new sailboard will cost about $1,000. Used ones are much cheaper.

Charters on well-equipped boats in the Caribbean usually start around $1,000 per person per week, not including food or airfare. Windjammer cruises start around $600 per person, including food.

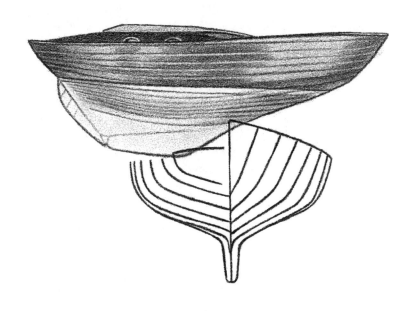

sailors, tinkering and puttering on board is as rewarding as shoving away from the dock.

In cross-section, the hull of a Folkboat is shaped like a wine glass. The ribs are thick stocks of wood bent to that shape, to which the planking or skin is attached. These ribs make two curves, in opposite directions. Getting wood to bend like that is difficult. Oak, which is generally used for ribs because of its strength, is particularly difficult.

The rib-building technique Armin showed me was to take a piece of oak two inches thick and slice it into four half-inch thick slices. We slathered the slices with epoxy glue, bent them into place against the compound curves of the hull, and drilled through them. We stuck bronze bolts through the planking and through the laminated ribs and turned them tight before the glue set. With 10 of these new ribs, the hull was probably stronger than when it was new. Later I was to learn the more traditional method of bending ribs—by heating them in steam until you can bend the wood like copper.

(God Bless Armin, who was one of the kindest persons I have ever met. Armin died on May 14, 1986, during the sinking of the *Pride of Baltimore*. He was skipper of the 157-foot topsail schooner, and had complained about her being top-heavy with sail. After returning from Europe, she capsized in a sudden squall near St. John's island in the Caribbean. Armin and some of the crew managed to swim clear of the rig. But Armin, with his selfless nature, swam back into the capsized rig to find the rest of the crew, and drowned.)

Once the Folkboat was ready, we launched her at Brownell's Boat Yard in Mattapoisett. Water gushed in through the cracks in the hull. I thought I had botched the ribs, but the old yard hands calmly stuck a few pumps in her and told me to come back tomorrow. Sure enough, when I returned, the hull was dry; the hull planks had swollen with moisture, sealing off the leaks.

The boatyard moved *Vaga* over to the town dock and said I could stay there until the next day. As I went about preparing for my first venture out to sea, a local lobsterman motored up in a giant lobsterboat and in no uncertain terms told me and my "sailboat" to move out of the way. Commercial fishermen are on the sea to earn a living, and have little respect for yachts and "play" sailors.

Terrified by this guy, I ran down below and grabbed my small outboard engine. Placing it in the brackets on the stern, I fumbled with the long pin that went through the pivot. The lobsterman yelled at me to hurry up, so I nervously figured that the engine would rest there just fine. I'd fit the pin through later.

I started the engine, slipped it into gear and moved away from the dock. Out of danger now, I slowed the engine down and SPLASH—it popped right off the stern and bubbled desperately as it sunk to the bottom of the harbor.

As soon as the propeller stopped pushing the boat, it dragged in the water and pulled the engine right off the stern—precisely what the pin was to prevent. Two kids on the dock started laughing hysterically. I was pissed, but I was also embarrassed. Luckily I had enough momentum to make it to the other dock, where I threw a line to a man staring at me with a paternal smile. Thankfully, he didn't say a word to me. He'd probably been there himself at one time.

When my friend Davie Allen arrived to help me sail *Vaga* to Nantucket, he howled at the story of my lost engine. Then he wanted to know what I had done to replace it. "Nothing," I said, "we'll sail over."

"Oh, no we won't," rejoined Davie, "I'm not going to get stuck out there for two days with no wind. Let's find it." Find it? It's at the bottom of the harbor. What good is it? As it turned out, my engine was a British Seagull, one of the mechanical marvels of this half-century. Seagulls are simple engines of low horsepower and low RPMs, designed to push a lot of weight at a slow speed. They are also designed to be repaired on the spot, and are famous for starting in the worst conditions, even after being dunked. It was worth trying, so we borrowed a dinghy and treble hook, and dragged back and forth over the spot where the engine went in. We were unsuccessful.

Nearly $500 later, with a shiny new Seagull on the stern, we shoved off for Nantucket. Davie was right. We didn't have a breath of wind the entire trip, and motored all the way.

Once I got the Folkboat to Nantucket, I became more confident and began sailing farther and farther. There was still much to learn, though.

One August afternoon, two English friends and I sailed out of the harbor and down the shore about a mile, where we anchored in front of the house where I was living. Another housesitting job, this one was on a 100-

foot bluff, with a white, wooden stairway leading down through thickets of wild roses onto the beach.

For some reason, I left the mainsail up while the boat rested at anchor. We swam 50 feet ashore and went up the stairway to make some sandwiches.

Suddenly, my neighbor was breathlessly beating on the front door.

"Your boat is sailing away. Come quick," he yelled. I ran out onto the front lawn to see my boat sailing away, perfectly trimmed, heading toward the public beach about a mile distant.

I glanced off every third stair at best and hit the beach at full stride. The boat had sailed about 200 yards down the beach, and my lungs were bursting by the time I got even with it. But I ran another 50 yards ahead of it and dove straight into the sea. It's amazing what adrenaline will do for you.

I swam out 50 yards, grabbed the side and hauled myself into the cockpit. I thought for sure someone was on board. Like a scene from the movie, *On The Beach*, the lines controlling the mainsail had tangled perfectly around the tiller, so that the sail was trimmed and the rudder held firm. Releasing all that and heading *Vaga* into the wind, I went forward and pulled up the anchor, only to find that one of the anchor flukes had impaled a large conch shell, preventing the anchor from digging into the sand. An unbelievable set of circumstances fortunately caused no damage, other than to my pride, and my lungs.

In 1976, I entered the first Opera House Cup on Nantucket, a race for wooden boats which is now an

Anchors

The beginning and end of every voyage belong to the anchor.
—Joseph Conrad

The first anchors were heavy rocks tied to ropes—effective but difficult to maneuver. Now, anchors work more through finesse than sheer weight. Anchors basically come in two types. Burying anchors dig into soft bottoms of sand, clay, or mud, and hook anchors catch the bottom and work best on grass, rock, or coral surfaces.

The lunch anchor could be any one of several types of anchors and is typically small and easy to maneuver. It could be a grapnel anchor with hooks, a foldable "octopus," a small Danforth, a small mushroom, or any other similarly portable anchor. Sailors use a lunch anchor on dinghies and to anchor a larger boat for a short period of time without the hassle of deploying a larger anchor.

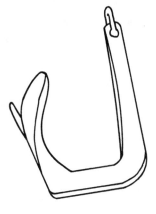

The Bruce anchor has no moving parts, can pivot 360 degrees when set and was first developed for use on North Sea oil rigs. A lightweight anchor somewhat similar to the plow, the Bruce works best on soft bottoms.

Probably the most popular small-boat anchor, the Danforth was invented by R.S. Danforth in 1939 and used on World War II landing craft. It stores flat and is relatively light. It holds particularly well in mud, sand, or clay but has difficulty maintaining a purchase on grassy or rocky bottoms.

The traditional kedge anchor has faded into virtual obsolescence because of its low weight to holding power ratio. As a hook-type anchor, though, it does have some utility on hard or vegetation-covered bottoms. It is also known as the yachtsman's or Herreshoff.

A sea anchor, also called a drogue, is usually made of cloth and acts like a seaborne parachute. Typically deployed in severe storms and therefore seldom on a day sailer, a sea anchor is used to slow the boat down or smooth out the ride by aligning the boat with the seas. A sea anchor does not come in contact with the bottom but instead streams in the water behind the boat.

Primarily used in permanent moorings, the mushroom anchor is usually deep in the mud below the buoys to which you tie your boat. Mushrooms need time to sink into soft bottoms and gain a good foothold and are therefore seldom used on cruising boats.

The plow or CQR ("secure") anchor often hangs off the bow of a boat and can be used in conjunction with a Danforth when setting multiple anchors. The plow also works best on soft bottoms into which it plows to bury itself. Cambridge professor G.I. Taylor invented the plow in 1933.

Note: Even if you pick the ideal anchor, it will not hold well without the correct angle of pull (scope). Adequate scope, usually five to seven times water depth, on the anchor rode is crucial to any anchor's effectiveness.

annual event with considerable prestige. Happily, the first race was very casual. Gwenn Guillard, owner of the Opera House restaurant on Nantucket, placed a minimum length requirement of 26 feet on the boats, but allowed me to tie a broom stick to *Vaga's* bow as a fake bowsprit.

The wind on the morning of the race was howling—25 to 30 knots—which the big boats loved. My crew—Debbie Jackson, who worked for Elin Anderwald at the Nantucket Sail Repair—bravely sailed with me through waves far too big for us. It was all we could do to get a half-full cup of coffee into the cockpit. Drinking it was another challenge. To add to our misery, as Sandy Clothier sailed past us on her father's handsome 68-foot ketch, she tantalizingly offered us a cocktail, which she held easily on a level deck heaving ever so slowly. We had the last laugh though; at the race party that night, Gwenn announced that on handicap, we had beat the big ketch.

That fall, as the air grew colder and the leaves changed color, I moved off the island and to a new job with the Associated Press in Boston.

I left *Vaga* on Nantucket that winter, and returned in the spring to bring her to the mainland. Twice the weather wouldn't cooperate and I had to fly back to Boston. On the third try in early May, after waiting two days for a storm to pass, I jumped on board and shoved off at around 2 P.M., for a six-hour sail to Hyannis. Gliding through the still very cold water, I felt great to be back on my boat. It would be wonderful to get her looking good, and to go sailing around Boston Harbor.

Having sailed to Hyannis several times before on other boats, I knew the basic general direction in which to get started. After about an hour, I looked for the charts to plot a course. In my haste to leave, I had left them on the dock.

I knew the general scheme of things, but in the dark it would be tough finding the exact buoys I needed. Still it had taken so long to start this trip, and I didn't want to turn back.

On I sailed into the darkness. After an eternity the lights of Cape Cod began showing up, but they were an indecipherable mess. Nothing looked familiar. I couldn't find any string of lighted buoys resembling a channel. I couldn't even find any red or green lights, which indicate the approach to a channel. Only white lights, which didn't tell me anything. Sailing east for about an hour, I finally saw a flashing red light, a large beacon which I reached 30 minutes later.

Against the featureless night, the huge size and tangible presence of the beacon scared me. Where the hell was I? Something triggered my memory, and I remembered that this was the beacon just west of the entrance into Hyannisport. Relief washed through me. I knew where I was. I knew I was going to get in that night. I looked at the beacon, maybe 15 feet tall, and now I felt reassured by its strength and presence. I settled into the cockpit, relaxed and in control. As I looked over my right shoulder, I saw a monstrously large full moon rising out of the water, transforming an ink-black sea into a glimmering, glistening sight. Not only was I going to get in that night—it was turning into a beautiful sail.

About two hours later, I entered the Hyannis channel. It was around 10 P.M., and I was cold and damp. The wind was very light inside the harbor. I had all sails up as I ghosted by Baxter's, a waterfront bar. Inside, the crowd laughed and drank, warm and chummy. I felt a twitch of loneliness, of being too independent and solo, and of wanting to belong.

"Are you Mike McPhee?" came a distant voice out of the dark.

I could make out a silhouette on the deck of Baxter's, leaning over the rail toward me.

"Yeah. How'd you know?"

"Your friends from Nantucket have been calling to keep a watch out for you. They found your charts."

The warmth of those two sentences evaporated my dampness and loneliness. What wonderful friends! I tied up at the dock in the bright moonlight, feeling happy and warm. It was hard to believe that just a short while before I had been so lost and scared.

The more I sailed my Folkboat in and out of all the little bays and estuaries around Nantucket and Cape Cod, the more I started gazing out to the watery horizon, wondering what it was like out there. Oh, I was sure the water didn't look any different, except that there would be no land in sight. But I couldn't imagine the frame of mind offshore sailing would create, when the entire world would consist of a boat small enough to jump across. The idea of being in a monster storm, of sliding down one monster wave and up in the next in a tiny boat, was more than I could envision.

The opportunity to find out about offshore sailing came more quickly than I expected, in the form of Alfie Sanford, one of the truly eccentric characters on Nantucket. About 40 years old, Alfie was wildly wealthy and equally smart, with degrees from Harvard and MIT. Alfie was slim and slight and even looked a little like Mr. Peepers, but in reality he was wiry and tough and probably one of the best sailors on the island.

Alfie and his wife Julie had watched me work on and sail my Folkboat. Sensing that I would like to learn more about sailing, they asked if I would be interested in joining them to bring a boat up from the Bahamas to Annapolis, Maryland. They would arrange for the plane tickets; I would need to get a seabag with a few shirts, shorts, and foulweather gear, and to be ready to go in two weeks. I didn't hesitate a moment, and said yes, without having a clue as to what I was getting into.

We flew into Miami, then boarded a puddle-jumper over to Nassau, in the Bahamas. I had an intoxicating night in Nassau, and the next morning, with a massive hangover, I got on the smallest plane I had ever seen, with no glass in the windows, for a 45-minute flight to Deadman Cay. We flew over brilliant, light blue water and pure white beaches, over endless shapes of little islands, coral reefs and sand shoals. You could almost see the ocean current by the shape of the sand shoals wrapping around the ends of the islands, leaving the narrowest of channels between them.

The boat was a handsome 42-foot yawl. Alfie's uncle had purchased the boat farther south and brought it up as far as their time would allow. We would bring it the rest of the way to Annapolis. Meeting us on board was Alfie's cousin, Sarah, who stayed on after her father left.

We provisioned the boat with lots of local fruits and vegetables, juice drinks, and water. There were already plenty of staples and canned meats.

The first thing I learned about ocean voyages is how thorough the preparations should be. Alfie was meticulous, in my view, overly so, in preparing the boat, and particularly the navigational equipment. I was to learn why. After topping off the fuel and making one last check of the safety and life-saving equipment, Alfie fired up the engine. I slacked off and untied the dock lines, and we were free— off into that huge expanse I had only imagined.

Actually, the first several hundred miles were spent weaving in and out of the Bahamas, a long scattering of oddly shaped islands beginning just east of Miami and extending southeast several hundred miles toward Haiti and the Dominican Republic. The Bahamas parallel the northern coast of Cuba, roughly 200 miles to the northeast.

We sailed around the clock, so we divided the crew into two watches: Alfie and Julie, Sarah and me. Each couple would be on watch for four hours, then off for four, through the day and through the night. Whoever was not steering could sleep, but only on deck where they could be wakened easily for sail trim or to take over the helm.

Our first moment of concern came at dawn the next day, as we tried to sail between Cat Island and Eleuthera.

With the sky just beginning to lighten, it was nearly impossible to distinguish where the land ended and the water began. There were several large coral beds off to starboard, and it was critical to know exactly where we were.

Alfie chose to start the engine, drop the sails and motor around for several hours until it was light enough to pick our passage: the first of many good seasmanship tactics I learned from him. On my own, I would have tried to inch my way in closer and closer until I could see the edge of land. Alfie was afraid of getting trapped by the coral and chose to know what he was getting into before he got underway.

We made it through the channel with no problem and continued winding our way up through the islands. I gradually became numb from the four-on, four-off routine through the nights; anticipating my next wake-up call in four hours, I never really got any good sleep. It was also too hot during the daytime and plus I didn't want to miss anything, like the supertanker anchored off Freeport, waiting to unload. Truly, the ship was as long as some of the islands we passed. And it was so wide, it must have taken us five minutes to sail across its bow. You just don't have any idea how big those things are until you see one up close.

We docked the next day in Freeport and replenished our provisions, water, and fuel. Our next stop would be Cape Hatteras, North Carolina, roughly 650 miles away.

As we shoved off into the Gulf Stream, a large current that flows northeast up the coast and out toward Labrador and Greenland. I steered intrepidly, somewhat awed by the entire undertaking. I shall never forget Alfie, standing at the nav station in the overalls of his foulweather suit, tying a loop of string around the end of his glasses so that they would dangle on his chest. He climbed into the cockpit, put his glasses on and announced, almost triumphantly, "Now! I am ready for anything the sea can throw at us." I'm sure it was a ritual he has performed at the start of every offshore passage, but I didn't know how to take it, or what might happen next.

As we left sight of land, Alfie began keeping track of our location through a process called "dead reckoning." Every four hours, Alfie noted our position with a little mark on the chart, along with our speed, wind speed, current, and any other observations. Having this record is invaluable if you become confused, which can happen easily as conditions change. By keeping track of little things, like drift, you begin to spot patterns, or repeating errors or inaccuracies that can have a significant effect over seven or ten days.

Life on an offshore boat quickly settles into a somewhat dull routine, but time goes by surprisingly fast. It's amazing how easily you can fill your days by reading, cooking, sleeping, steering, and sometimes swimming.

As we sailed out into the Sargasso sea, which is more than three miles deep and a dark indigo-blue color, the wind dropped to a mere whisper. Four dolphins came alongside and actually performed for our cheers, seemingly jumping more frequently out of the water the louder we clapped and yelled.

Roasting in the heat, I asked Alfie about dropping a

line off the stern and swimming behind the boat. I wanted to see if I could swim with the dolphins, in their natural habitat. The boat was sailing at only two knots, so Alfie said it would be OK. I donned fins, a mask, and a snorkel and went overboard, clutching a line tied to the stern.

What a spooky feeling! The depth and darkness of the water frightened me. The distance to land, more than 200 miles, frightened me. And the thought of the dolphins frightened me as well, although I wanted to see if they would approach me. I feared them not for their attitude, which had appeared friendly and playful, but for their strength and speed. I was in their territory, and completely vulnerable should something go wrong.

Despite all my fears, I stayed in the water for nearly half an hour. I gradually calmed down about the depth and the distance. I saw one tiny little striped fish, no bigger than a tablespoon, that was hiding behind the propeller, hitching a ride by drafting our boat! Alas, the dolphins never returned.

The weather stayed calm and generally provided us with easy sailing and great tans. Occasional storms would blow by and sometimes wash us with short, torrential downpours. One night, around midnight, I had the helm when the wind began to crank up. I sensed no urgency, other than an increase in speed, but Alfie woke and came on deck. After one look around he told me to get my foulweather gear on quickly, and went below to do just that. What did he see? Feeling some alarm, but not panic, I gave Sarah the wheel and put on all my gear.

Alfie came back on deck and pointed to roughly 10 o'clock. Although it was nearly pitch dark, I began to make out some angry clouds right down on the water. Alfie said it was a line squall headed our way. He warned that the winds would pick up violently, then change direction 90 degrees.

Alfie and I quickly ran to the bow, dropped the genoa, and secured it tightly to the deck. Back in the cockpit, Alfie ordered the mainsail let out so that once the wind started the pocket would luff halfway back on the sail.

Suddenly, out of nowhere, the clouds roared right into us, rain started falling heavily and the wind picked up to roughly 50 or 55 miles an hour. Just as Alfie had predicted, the wind had backed around a full 90 degrees and was howling from the other side. Thirty minutes ago we were on a pleasant nighttime drift. Now we were in full foulweather gear, rain and spray streaking down our faces, and the boat, with only the mainsail straining, was heeled well over and charging through foaming waves and spray.

Never did we panic or lose control. Alfie had spotted the storm where I had seen nothing. He knew what to expect and how to prepare for it. The storm happened exactly as he had predicted; we were ready and rode it out. Although the ride was wild, I never once felt we were being overwhelmed or even overpowered. Ah, the wisdom of experience.

Suddenly, the lightning started. Huge white bolts streaked out of the sky directly into the black water, maybe a quarter of a mile away. The sky would light up, the waves would become visible for an instant and then

only the white streak would remain in my vision, like a light turned off that I could still see. Then another bolt. I could see the silhouettes of the rigging and the mast for an instant, and the churning sea surrounding us.

Alfie told us to look at the top of the masts. St. Elmo's fire! A strange green glow was forming like a dull light off the top of the masts and the radio antenna. It looked as if the masts were very dim flashlights, emitting a weak green light. St. Elmo's fire is legendary for having scared the daylights out of early sailors, in the days before electron transfer was understood. It's caused by the transfer of negatively charged ions into air that is positively charged. In a sense, it's a very weak form of electricity, acting similarly to lightning.

Just then, the granddaddy of all lightning bolts let loose out of the sky, directly in front of us. The bolt split into five fingers and curved directly toward us. I saw five orange balls leading the bolts. The lightning shot out over the top of the mast, and lit up the sky like a stadium. It was an awesome display. Years later, a man at the National Oceanic and Atmospheric Administration told me that this form of lightning, with the orange balls, is extremely rare.

The storm blew past us and soon the sea began to calm. We raised the genoa again and resumed our course. Alfie and Julie started their watch, I went below to my bunk, amazed and in awe of nature. I was beginning to understand the attraction of the sea.

The trip continued without mishap. A few more storms blew in but none of consequence. Our last night out the wind blew over 25 knots. That was manageable

and propelled us along at a good clip. Eventually, the waves grew into sizeable rollers, big swells that don't break and, if you're going in the same direction, can be fun trying to surf down.

We had been out for 10 days and I was looking forward to getting on land. At the helm, I had improved at reading the stars, and was attempting to steer by them and not the compass. I was also enjoying the rollers and occasionally managing to steer over one and surf down it, hitting 9 or 10 knots before the wave would pass us by and leave us in the trough.

Suddenly, exactly dead ahead, I spotted the sweeping beacon of the lighthouse on Cape Hatteras. We were directly on course and here was the proverbial light in the window—the end of a magnificent trip, the first of many.

A SAILING PRIMER
Sailing Terminology

At first look, a sailboat may seem complex and intimidating. But everything on a sailboat has a purpose and is designed to perform as efficiently as possible. Most sailboat equipment has evolved over decades of solving the same problems over and over. As with automobiles, many of the breakthroughs have been generated through the racing side of the sport, and then adapted for general use.

Sailing has its own language, so let's start with the correct names. (Learning to talk a good game of sailing sometimes is harder than getting the boat to go fast.)

Some names have obvious origins, others are obscure. Many terms are derivations formed over centuries of sailing, and may seem strange. A good example is that there are no ropes on a sailboat; instead, there are lines, sheets, halyards, rodes, guys, and preventers. This to prevent the skipper constantly yelling, "Grab that rope over there. No, not that one, the next one, no, not that far, the one next to it." Instead, he or she only has to yell, "Grab the starboard jib sheet!"— a specific item.

BOATS

The front, sharp end of the boat is the **bow**. There is no left or right on a boat, because as soon as you turn your body 180 degrees around, what was on your left is now on

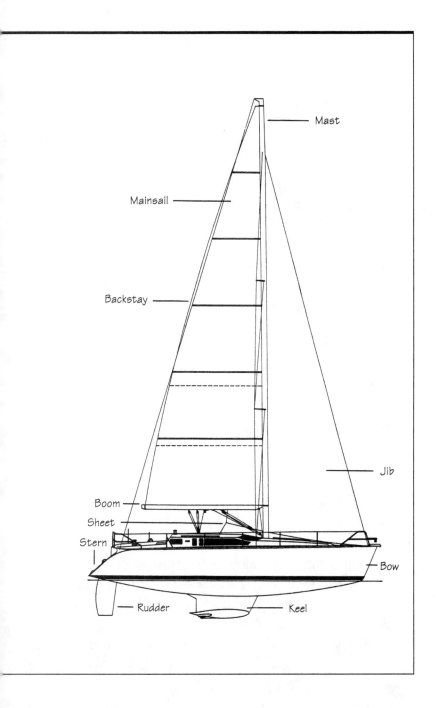

Mast

Mainsail

Backstay

Jib

Boom

Sheet

Stern

Bow

Rudder

Keel

your right. So directions are always given from the skipper's viewpoint, facing forward. Looking toward the bow, the left side is **port**, and the right is **starboard**.

This comes from the old Scandinavian sailboats that were steered with a steering board over the right side. That name evolved into starboard. To keep from damaging the steering board, they always docked on the left or port side. A trick to keeping the two terms straight is to remember that both port and left have four letters.

The rear of the boat is the **stern**, and the sides of the boat are the **beam**, either port or starboard beam. The width of the boat is also referred to as the beam, as in narrow beam. You walk **forward** to the bow, or **aft** to the stern. If you stop in the middle, you're **amidship**. That's where you always end up when you're learning, so I guess that's why the naval academy students are called midshipmen.

The **spars** support the sails. The tall spar extending vertically in the center of the boat is the **mast**. Attached to the mast at a 90-degree angle, extending horizontally toward the stern, is the **boom**, probably the most appropriately named item for the times when it swings across the deck and hits you on the head.

The **mainsail**, the largest sail, is attached to the mast and boom. The small triangular sail up front on the bow is the **jib**. A large jib is a **genoa**. The large balloonlike sail, often in vivid, contrasting colors, is the **spinnaker**.

The **rudder** extends into the water near the stern to steer the boat. The **tiller**, or wheel, if the boat has a wheel, moves the rudder.

All the ropes and wires and cables are generically called

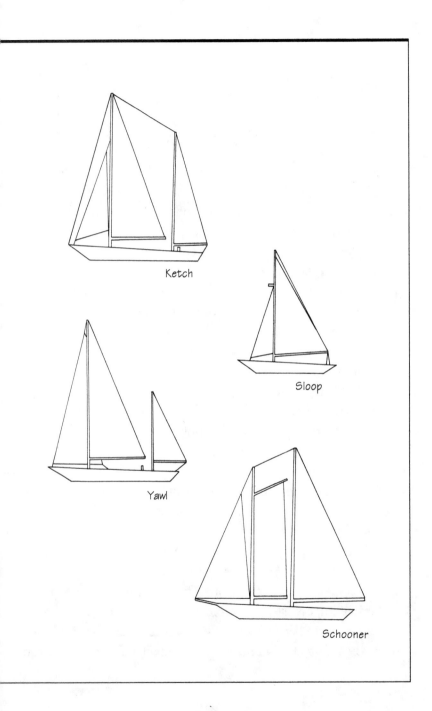

Ketch

Sloop

Yawl

Schooner

the **rigging**. There are two kinds of rigging—**standing**, which doesn't move, and **running**, which the crew adjusts when sailing. The standing rigging is usually made of wire cable and holds up the masts: the **forestay**, which runs from the bow to the top of the mast; the **backstay**, which runs from the stern to the top of the mast; and the **sidestays** . . . you guessed it. Sidestays are sometimes called **shrouds**. Larger boats have much more standing rigging, particularly boats with two or more masts.

The running rigging consists of the lines that work the sails. A **halyard** runs up the mast, around a pulley and down to the top of the sail. Pulling on the halyard raises the sail. There are separate halyards for the jib, the mainsail, the spinnaker, or any other sails on the boat.

To pull the sail in against the wind, you use the **sheet** tied to the trailing corner of the sail or boom. Thus, you **sheet in** a sail. There are separate port and starboard sheets for the jib and spinnaker, because they have to go on either side of the mast. The mainsail usually has only one sheet.

If a boat has one mast, it is a **sloop**. If it has two masts, it can be one of three common designs: if the aft or **mizzen** mast is shorter than the forward mast, it is a **ketch** or a **yawl**. It's a ketch if the mizzen mast is forward of the rudder and a yawl if the mizzen mast is aft of the rudder. (Remember, "k" comes before "y".) If, however, the aft mast is taller than the forward mast, the boat is a **schooner**.

These distinctions may sound like organized confusion, but they are important, because the size and placement of the masts cause boats to handle differently. Sloops and yawls are fast going upwind. Ketches, with a smaller mainsail and a larger mizzen sail than a yawl, go much better downwind, and generally don't heel over as much as a sloop or a yawl because the main mast is not as tall. Larger sails are more efficient in the wind, but harder for a small crew to manage.

Schooners generally are bigger boats and carry a lot of sail for power or speed. However, the increase in sail area is broken down into a greater number of sails, usually a minimum of four or five. This enables a smaller crew to handle a lot of sail. It also gives the crew more combinations of sails to fly during a storm.

WIND

The wind is always named for the direction it is coming from, not the direction it is going to. Therefore, an easterly breeze is coming from the east. Sailboats are powered by the wind, and once again, it's important to be able to describe the wind, regardless of the direction of the boat.

Anything upwind, or facing the wind, is **to windward** or **to weather**. Another boat upwind from you is to windward of you. The side of your boat that the wind is hitting is the windward side or weather side. The side of an island that the wind is blowing against is the windward or weather shore.

Conversely, anything downwind, or facing away from the wind, is **to leeward** (pronounced loo'erd) or the **lee** side. Thus, a boat downwind is to leeward, the side of your boat not facing the wind is the leeward or lee side. Similarly, the protected side of an island, out of the wind, is the leeward or lee shore. Another usage is to sail into the lee of an island to get out of the wind.

POINTS OF SAIL

Zigzagging up into the wind is called **tacking** or **beating** to windward. Sailing downwind is **running**. This is when some boats raise their spinnakers, those big colorful sails designed to hold as much wind as possible. Sailing with the wind 90 degrees to the side, with the sails halfway out, is **reaching**.

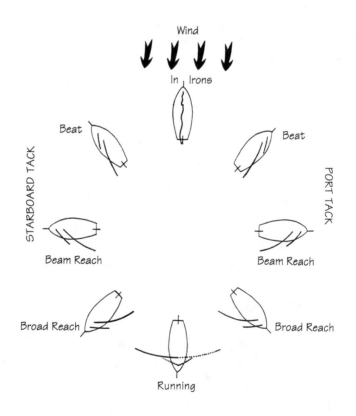

Telltales

Most sailors need help determining the wind direction, and do it with telltales, which come in a variety of forms. The most common method for creating telltales is to tape six-inch pieces of yarn or recording tape on both sides of the leading edge of the jib. Tape one pair about six feet off the deck, and another pair about six feet below the head of the sail. When both telltales flow straight back, the airflow on both sides of the sail is uninterrupted, the sail is trimmed perfectly to the wind and is at maximum efficiency. Other telltales can be taped to the side shrouds. Some sailors also use a mechanical windvane at the masthead. □

How Sailboats Sail

When sailing downwind, the sails are set out to the side and the **following** wind simply pushes the boat along, like a leaf on the water.

Sailing upwind, however, involves three forces: the thrust generated by the airfoil effect of the sails, the weight of ballast controlling the angle of heel of the boat, and the leeway imposed by the movement of the keel or centerboard through the water.

The airfoil principle allows a sailboat to go into the wind, an airplane to fly, and a Frisbee to hover. In cross-section, the bottom of an airplane wing is flat, and the top is curved. As the airplane moves, the air passing over the top of the wing travels a longer distance—and therefore faster—than the air passing underneath the wing. As a result, air pressure (nominally 14.7 pounds per square inch at sea level) on top of the wing is reduced, generating a condition known as **lift**—the wing rises.

When moving into the wind, a sail is a vertical airfoil. Sails are not flat, but bellied in a shape exactly like the arc of an airplane wing. A sail doesn't have a second, underneath or bottom surface like a wing, because it must be able to flop over onto the other side and form another arc, a mirror image.

The force created by an airfoil forms at right angles (90 degrees) to the wind—fine for an airplane which needs upward lift, but not so good for a sailboat which wants to move ahead into the wind. If the boat and sail are in line with the wind (as with an airplane wing) the force generated by the sail will be perpendicular to the boat, and will only try to tilt the boat over. But if you let the sails out just a little, that force is then directed slightly forward, say to 10 o'clock if the boat is sailing toward 12 o'clock. It's that little bit of forward pull that the boat takes advantage of.

To get the sails to fill with wind and belly out, the boat must turn slightly away from the wind. Then, to get the sails pulling slightly forward, the boat must turn even further off the wind. This adds up to about 45 degrees, which is about the closest a boat can sail into the wind. Thus, to reach a position which is upwind, a boat sails 45 degrees to the left of the wind for awhile, then **tacks** over to 45 degrees to the right of the wind for about the same length of time, then back again to the left.

Sailing upwind is difficult if not impossible without a keel or centerboard. While part of the force created by the sail wants to pull the boat forward, a larger part of the force wants to pull the boat over sideways. This is called **heel**.

To keep a sailboat upright it must have counterweighting **ballast**. Keelboats have ballast built into the keel, usually in the form of a large bulb of heavy metal, such as lead or iron, bolted to the bottom. As the boat heels over, the keel rises on the opposite side underwater. The higher it rises, the more force it takes to keep it up. At the same time, and conversely, the farther a sailboat heels over, the less force the sails generate, because the wind begins spilling off the tops of the sails. When the sails and keel reach equilibrium the boat will remain at a steady angle of heel.

Sailboats are designed to heel over quite far, usually to

the point where water washes up on the deck. It's exciting to sail rail underwater. If the boat is designed properly, only two things will sink it—water coming in through a hatch or an opening, or a wave pushing it over. This happens rarely, and only in severe storms.

On the average, 50 percent of all sailing is done to windward, heeling over. For maximum efficiency when sailing in this position, designers used to believe it was best to make the hull as slim and skinny as possible, and fit it with a heavy, deep keel. Boats of this type do well in heavy weather, and are safe, but can be very slow in light air. Today, the trend in boat design is toward lighter, wider hulls. These have much less tendency to heel, and thus can use lighter, shallower keels. The catch is that the wider hull must still be able to slide efficiently through the water, and this depends on the quality and sophistication of the hull design.

On a boat with a centerboard, the crew is the ballast. To balance the right angle force generated by the sail, the crew sits up on the weather rail, the windward side. If the boat still wants to tip over, the crew must **hike out** on harnesses attached to the top of the mast, so they can lean straight out over the water for maximum leverage against the wind. It can be an athletic business, and from my experience, permanent ballast is much more reliable!

Keelboats are self-righting; if knocked flat, then, provided there's not too much water in the hull, the weight of the keel will pull the boat upright again. Centerboard boats which tip over generally are designed to be righted after bailing out by the crew. Many of them have flotation, built-in blocks of foam or other buoyant materials, that keeps them from sinking. The crew can climb back in, finish bailing it out, and continue sailing.

A keel or centerboard also acts to counter **leeway,** where the wind and the lift of the sail push the boat sideways. The ability of a keel or centerboard to keep a boat on track is a function of surface area and shape, and, in the case of a keel, weight—the more vertical the keel, the more side surface area it presents. Thus, a keelboat which is running rail under will present less effective keel surface, and will have to be steered more upwind, because the boat will have a greater tendency to slide sideways through the water.

Displacement boats displace water as they move forward. **Planing** boats plane over the top of the water as they move forward. The most basic example of a planing vessel is a windsurfer, a surfboard with a sail on it. These skim along the top of the water with little effort. Some daysailers plane, such as the Laser and the Sunfish. And as the large ocean-racing boats become lighter and lighter, many are now able to plane down the sides of waves, reaching frightfully fast speeds.

Although planing boats ride on top of, rather than in, the water, they are subject to the same physical principles as displacement boats. The windsurfer hikes out to counteract the sideways thrust of the sail, and the board uses a dagger-like **fin** to track against leeway. On larger vessels, the keel or centerboard—sometimes also called a fin—produces the same effect. □

Sizing Up a Boat

In comparing boats, there are certain dimensions that quickly give you a rough sketch of the hull shape and tell you if the boat is a cruiser, a racer, or if it was designed with some specific purpose in mind.

The first dimension always is LOA, or length overall. This is the length of the boat from the farthest point forward, whatever it is, to the farthest point aft, whatever that might be. Some boats have long bowsprits or boomkins, which are included in LOA.

The second dimension is LOD, or length on deck. This eliminates bowsprits, boomkins, and reverse stern counters, and tells exactly how far you can walk around on a boat.

The next dimension is LWL, or length of waterline, where the hull meets the water. LWL is a critical dimension because the top speed of displacement sailboats, those that displace water as they move compared to planing sailboats (such as a Hobie Cat) that skim across the water, is limited by the length of their waterline. The formula is: the square root of the LWL multiplied by 1.34 equals the hull speed in knots. Hull speed is defined as the maximum efficient speed a displacement hull can reach.

The next dimension is the beam, or widest width of the boat. Width to length ratios tell you a lot about the stability of a boat. Older racing boats were very skinny, 5:1 and 6:1, with a lot of ballast in a deep keel. Newer racing boats have much lower ratios, 4:1 or 3:1, for good stability with less ballast. This results in a lighter boat.

The displacement of a boat is a calculated by measuring

the weight of water it displaces. Today, as racing boats approach planing speeds, the D/L (displacement/waterline-length) ratio tells a designer or buyer the planing ability of a boat. Cruising boats have D/L ratios in the 500:1 to 600:1 range. Racing boats slim down to the 300:1 range. The ultra light displacement boats (ULDB), euphemistically referred to as "sleds," have a ratio of 110:1 or less.

Ballast is a measurement of the amount of weight placed in the keel to stabilize the boat. The ballast and beam together give the buyer an idea of how "tender" or tippy the boat will be going to windward.

Finally, the sail area, usually reckoned by measuring the mainsail and a jib that would fill the foretriangle with no overlap, tells how much power the boat has. The sail area of a boat normally does not include a spinnaker or any oversized sails like a genoa or reacher.

Designers use all these measurements to determine how a boat will handle in light winds, heavy winds, offshore in big seas, in shallow bays, or wherever the boat will be used most of the time. Racers also use these measurements to handicap the boats in a fleet, so that theoretically at least, different types of boats race on even terms, and winning is down to the sailing abilities of the skippers and crews. □

Materials

HULLS

Wood was the first material for hulls. It was used not because it floats, but because of its availability and the ease with which it can be shaped and fastened together. The primary disadvantages of wood are that it rots, can break, and, compared to modern materials, is relatively heavy.

Fiberglass, when it was introduced in the 1950s, became extremely popular because it is rot- and leak-free and relatively light. It does, however, weep or sweat, which can be more annoying than leaks. It deteriorates in ultraviolet rays of the sun but can be refinished easily.

At first, fiberglass, or GRP (glass-reinforced polyester) was hailed as maintenance-free. Then it was discovered that unattended fiberglass would gradually become porous, and by osmosis, soak up water. The phenomenon was discovered when it proved impossible for boatyard cranes to lift certain GRP yachts out of the water, because they had increased four or five times in weight! Today, knowledgeable owners of GRP yachts regularly service their hulls.

In the 1960s, ferrocement created some excitement. In this boat building process, the hull shape was formed with steel mesh and reinforcing rods, which were then heavily coated with a very fine concrete. Cement hulls are inexpensive to make but heavy. They fell out of favor after a decade because owners couldn't finish their boats off in "yacht" fashion. No matter how many coats of paint or strips of wood trim were added, concrete hulls always looked like, well, concrete.

Metal hulls have proven very able and seaworthy—steel, despite its propensity for corrosion in salt water; and aluminum, despite its being difficult to work with. Generally, metal hulls are limited to boats intended for use in severe conditions, and larger boats.

Wood hulls, of a sort, have reclaimed some of their lost popularity—in a new form known as cold-molded. These hulls are made of strips of wood veneer less than 1/4 inch thick, lathered in epoxy resin and laid up in strips—some longitudinal, some latitudinal and some diagonal—a technique similar to the making of papier mâché figures from strips of newspaper and flour glue. These boats retain the look of wood, but are thinner and lighter, yet are stronger than fiberglass hulls. Also, because the wood is impregnated with epoxy, the hulls will not rot.

Today, composite hulls of Mylar, Kevlar, and now carbon fiber are the vogue for those who can afford them. These composites, used in a variety of methods such as sandwiched with balsa wood, honeycomb fiberboard, and polyurethane foam, have spawned a whole new era in ocean racing—the ultralights. These are long keelboats designed to get up and plane whenever possible, particularly down the slope of a wave. Racing speeds of 18 and 19 knots are not unheard of.

Carbon hulls are incredibly light. In a boat-building yard, three men can manage an 80-foot carbon hull—push it around on rollers, and even turn it over. If made of wood, an 80-foot hull would weigh around 20 tons!

One final technology being perfected in hull making is a new building technique, called pre-preg. Ordinarily, the resins in fiberglass, or any type of glue used to form a composite hull, are usually a two-part chemical that hardens a short while after the two parts are mixed. Building requires laying out whatever cloth, veneer, or binder being used, mixing the glue, and then setting it in place before it hardens. This technique, known as "wet," is messy, time-consuming, and labor-intensive.

Pre-preg composite materials use heat-sensitive hardeners. This allows the resins to be applied to the cloths or composite fabrics in a controlled situation at the factory, with uniform thickness and density. The materials, which are dry and easy to handle, are fitted onto a hull mold, then heated until they harden. Some yards also place composite hulls in a large vacuum to suck out any air trapped between layers and ensure a tight, uniform bonding.

SAILS

Since the days of the ancient Egyptians, sails were sewn of flax and cotton. Even as the size of ships increased in the eighteenth and nineteenth centuries, cotton canvas sails remained the standard.

During the 1930s, artificial fabrics began to appear, some with success. Rayon was first used in 1937 on the J-boat *Ranger*, considered by many to be the finest American J-boat ever built. Nylon appeared just after WWII. Its light weight made it ideal for spinnakers, but it stretched too much to be used for hard-sheeted windward sails.

In 1953, Dacron rapidly became the cloth of choice for sails. It was lighter and stronger than cotton, did not stretch much and was resistant to water and rot. Dacron is still the primary sail cloth today. It is very susceptible to the ultraviolet rays in sunlight, and should be kept covered when not in use.

In the early 1970s, Mylar came into use. Made from polyester film, Mylar can be combined with resin to form a fabric, woven into other fabrics like Dacron, or sandwiched with two layers of another fabric. It has much greater strength than Dacron, and less stretch, and it won't rot.

Ten years later, Kevlar appeared as the ultimate no-stretch, high strength, lightweight sail cloth. Kevlar is an artificial fiber developed by the Du Pont Company, and is used in a similar way as Mylar. Kevlar loses its strength rapidly when folded, thus has limitations, particularly in cruising boats. It is used primarily in the more expensive classes of racing boats, where performance is more important than economy or endurance.

The shape of sails has changed somewhat, but nothing like the changes in materials. The earliest sails were called lateen rigs—triangular sails with the longest dimension as the leading edge facing skyward, and the shortest dimension along the deck. The leading edge was attached to a spar, which was lashed to the mast. A small triangular section of the sail extended forward of the mast, serving like a jib to balance the aft portion of the sail. Boats with lateen rigs can only jibe, not tack, because the spar has to be stood up vertically, carried to the other side of the mast and lashed in that position. Lateen rigs are actually fairly efficient going to windward, and are still used in the Middle East on Arab dhows. Two of the most popular daysailers today, the Sunfish and the Sunflower, also use lateen rigs.

Lateen rigs gave way to square sails, which are more efficient downwind. Fore-and-aft sails were used as headsails, and occasionally on the aft mast.

As mariners learned more about ocean passages and prevailing winds, more of their sailing could be done downwind. Thus, the emphasis on square-rigged ships. Commerce or "trade" was carried by these ships. They followed the prevailing winds, hence the term "trade winds."

Trade winds are the reason Maine was nicknamed "Down East." Coastal schooners in the late 1800s didn't sail *up* to Maine, but headed east, which was *down*wind, because the prevailing winds were out of the southwest.

Square-rigged sails worked well downwind. But if a ship left the trade winds and wanted to work upwind, it was at a severe disadvantage. At best, square-riggers could point 60 degrees into the wind. Smaller ships, particularly coastal schooners and the burgeoning group of recreational yachts, had much more need for windward efficiency, and they focused on improving the fore-and-aft rigs.

The early mainsails and mizzensails were gaff-rigged—a square sail placed fore-and-aft with the yardarm attached to the top of of the mast and extending aft. Gradually, the gaff, or upper spar, was shortened to make for easier sail handling. Finally around 1920, a group of racers in Bermuda eliminated the gaff, extended the mast higher and hoisted a triangular sail. This modern-day Bermuda rig proved to be more efficient to windward because the design eliminated the twist in the upper portion of the sail. To carry the same amount of sail as a gaff rig, a Bermuda rig had to be much taller, which made it better for light air. The Bermuda rig gave away a slight downwind advantage in comparison to the gaff rig, but the compromise was worth it.

In the late 1920s, racers began experimenting with larger headsails, pulling them farther aft of the mast. Genoas are named for their first documented appearance at a 6-Meter regatta in Genoa, Italy.

Spinnakers appeared right after World War II with the advent of lightweight nylon. As more synthetic fabrics began to appear, emphasis was on the fabric. Successive synthetic fabrics have reduced weight and added strength. Today, computer-aided design is used to stretch lines of sails, to minimize give and optimize shape and performance. □

Lighting

Sailing at night is quite different from driving at night, primarily because there are no marked lanes or roads. It is important to be able to see another vessel, and it's equally important to see in what direction that vessel is headed. Airplanes have the same problem.

Whether it's a boat or an airplane, the port side has a red light, the starboard side a green light, and the stern has a white light, which can not be seen forward. I keep this straight by remembering that port wine is red. These port and starboard lights can be seen only from straight ahead to 90 degrees off their respective sides of the vessel. In other words, if the sailboat is headed exactly straight at you, you see both red and green. If you are 90 degrees or less off the port side of a boat, you see only a red light. If you are more than 90 degrees off either side, you see only the white stern light.

So, if you see both a red and green, the other vessel is headed straight at you. If the green light starts to fade and goes out of sight, leaving only the red light, the vessel is going to pass to your left, because you're looking at his left side. The opposite is true if the red light fades and the green light remains. That vessel is going to pass on your right side, so you should steer left. What light will the other vessel then see? He'll see your green, too.

If you think you've got it figured out, here's a little tongue twister for you to remember:

When green and red I see ahead,
I turn to starboard and show my red:
Green to green, red to red,
Pefect safety—go ahead.

But if to starboard red appear
It is my duty to keep clear.
To act as judgment says is proper:
To port or starboard, back or stop her. ☐

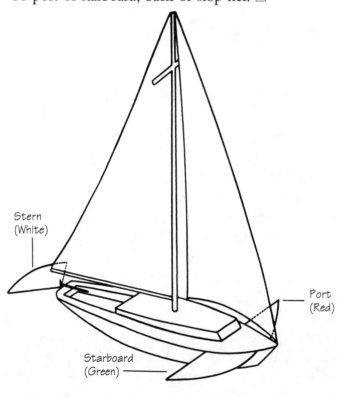

Stern
(White)

Port
(Red)

Starboard
(Green)

Equipment

There is a whole world out there of boat equipment and accessories—some of it is necessary, some of it is frivolous, and most all of it is expensive. In all fairness, some of the expense is warranted. Sailing hardware can be put under severe loads and must be exceptionally strong. A lot of equipment, however, is grossly overpriced, solely because it's going on a "yacht." Sailboat equipment is in the same class as medical equipment: some of the expense is warranted, some prices prey on the situation.

ROPES

Ropes were originally made of natural fibers: sisal, hemp, flax and manila. Generally, they served well, but by today's standards they stretched too far, were rough on the hands, chafed easily and swelled when wet, to the point of jamming in pulleys and sheaves.

Today, ropes are made primarily of polyester, either stranded or double braided. These ropes stretch very little, are not affected by water and are resistant to chafing. Nearly all the running rigging on a sailboat is made of polyester line.

In some of the bigger racing boats, polyester lines have Kevlar woven into them, to further reduce stretching. Here, cost is a limiting factor.

Polypropylene line is very inexpensive, relatively strong for its size, and floats in water, which makes it good for life-saving equipment and for fishing nets and bouys. However, it chafes easily, weakens in sunlight and is rough on your hands.

Nylon is preferred for anchors and dock lines primarily because it stretches. Boats frequently jerk their mooring and dock lines when hit by wakes or waves, and the stretch in nylon reduces shock.

DINGHIES

Dinghies are a must for cruising, where one of the real joys is to sail to some island or beach, anchor and row ashore for a picnic and swim. Dinghies are usually about eight-feet long and made of fiberglass. Most often they are simply rowed, but many have a mount for a small outboard engine. Some are equipped with sailing rigs, which are pretty inefficient but just fine for getting ashore. Inflatable dinghies, although expensive, work well because they won't damage your boat, can be deflated and stored for long passages, and are lightweight and sturdy. With a hard bottom and a rigid transom, they are capable of holding a powerful outboard engine for faster speeds and greater distances. □

Navigational Equipment

Equipment for determining the position of a boat is a category of its own, and today it involves some very sophisticated hardware, including satellites.

In the old days, sailors located their position by using a sextant to measure the angle of the sun or stars at precise times. Through trigonometry, the boat's position could be determined fairly accurately, usually within several miles.

Radar is useful in foggy or stormy areas or when offshore. Radar sends out a signal that bounces off an object and returns to the receiver. The time the signal takes to return is measured and translated into the distance the object is from the radar set.

Radar equipment is relatively expensive, usually more than $2,000, and can be finicky and temperamental. It also requires some practice to operate correctly. However, in fog or rain, radar can be indispensable for finding the shore, a buoy, or another boat. Many sailors have found themselves hopelessly lost a mere quarter-mile from shore and very grateful to the radar-equipped fisherman who happened by to lead them into the harbor.

During World War II, engineers developed the radio direction finder (RDF) which beeps as the operator tunes the directional antenna in on a radio signal. You draw a line on the chart from the known location of the radio signal out the same compass bearing that the antenna is pointed. Then you do the same with another radio station as close to 90 degrees from the first station as possible. The line where the two intersect is your approximate location. If only one radio station can be picked up, you draw a line from the radio station 180 degrees opposite the direction the RDF is giving. Your position is somewhere along that line. In such cases, you can sometimes use your depth sounder to measure the depth of water under your hull, and then find that depth on the RDF line, which will give you your exact location. RDF systems are still used, but not often.

Today, there are three main radio wave systems for determining position: Loran, or long range aid to navigation; SatNav, or satellite navigation; and GPS, or global positioning system.

Loran has been around the longest, since about the mid-1960s, and, because it works so well, it has become enormously popular. It is definitely the little guy's answer to weekend navigational worries because, for less than $500, a sailor can pinpoint his position to within one-quarter of a mile.

Loran involves "master" and "slave" transmitter stations located on land along both coasts. The receiver on the boat picks up a signal and measures the time differential of the signal between the two slave stations. It then calculates a "line of position" between the two stations, which can be read off a navigational chart. The same is done with another signal from another pair of slave stations, giving a second "line of position." Where the two lines cross is your location. Because the transmitters are permanently positioned on land, Loran is exceptionally accurate when used to return to a known position, such as a channel marker or a buoy that you marked on the way out. I once accompanied some lobstermen on a trip off Nantucket.

We motored all night, 120 miles out to sea. At dawn, the Loran brought us right up to a single bamboo pole used to mark one end of the lobster trawl.

The disadvantage of Loran is that the transmitters are land-based, with a range of about 1,000 miles. Large areas are not serviced by Loran. This is where SatNav takes over.

Originally developed by the U.S. Navy as the Transit system for its nuclear submarines, SatNav uses a signal sent from a satellite orbiting the poles of the earth. The receiver listens to the satellite's signal for two minutes. Using the satellite's position, which is transmitted continuously, and by using the Doppler effect, or the change in frequency of the radio signal, the SatNav calculates a line of position every two minutes. In 12 to 15 minutes, about six lines of position can be calculated, giving a very accurate position.

Disadvantages are that SatNav must take into account the vessel's speed and direction. Slight errors can result in a large positional error. And, although there are 13 Transit satellites in orbit, seven operational and six spares, there can be gaps of coverage when a satellite is too low to the horizon or below the horizon. It may take 90 minutes to several hours before another satellite appears. Perhaps the biggest disadvantage is the government's plan to discontinue Sat-Nav by 1996, to be replaced by GPS.

The advantage of GPS is that it will have 21 satellites operating continuously at very high altitudes in six orbital planes. At any time, anywhere in the world, at least four satellites will be in view. Because of the high orbits, a satellite will remain in view for 12 hours during each pass.

GPS does not use the Doppler effect. The receiver measures the time it takes a signal from a satellite to reach it. It knows when the signal was transmitted because all GPS receivers are synchronized with the satellites. Another satellite can be used by airplanes to determine altitude.

GPS is proving to be so reliable that Japanese carmakers are equipping some cars with GPS navigational systems that show a map on a screen in the car, along with the car's position. A similar system is becoming available for boats, and is already in use on some experimental craft, like *Amoco Procyon*. Some aircraft can be automatically landed with GPS, usually with an accuracy of several inches.

Disadvantages of GPS are its cost, beginning around $2,000, although that is falling rapidly as it becomes more popular; and the fact that the government, which uses the system for military equipment, can shut out all civilians, as it did during the Persian Gulf War in 1990. However, as the system is improved, the military is expected to develop its own set of signals, and should no longer interfere with civilians.

ELECTRONICS

The advent of microchips has made a wide assortment of electronic instruments available to the yachtsman. Here, we enter a world that separates not the men from the boys but the big spenders from those who would rather (or must) rely on their sailing skills. Some skippers are gadget freaks and have everything imaginable to help them sail their boat more efficiently. Other skippers shun elaborate equipment and prefer to rely on their own skills and instincts. It's less a matter of right or wrong, and more a question of style.

The most basic piece of electronic equipment is a radio, preferably a VHF radio, with crystals for the most common marine frequencies. The Coast Guard monitors channel 16, which is used for hailing aid during an emergency. Channel 16 is also used by mariners to hail other boats. Once contact is made, the two boats switch to another channel to continue conversation. VHF radios can be purchased for around $100 to $1,000. Antennas, cables, and mounts are extra. Another radio frequently found on many boats is the citizens' band, or CB radio. The Coast Guard also monitors CB frequencies.

The next pieces of electronic equipment most frequently found on boats are depth sounders and knot meters. Depth sounders give the skipper the depth of the water from the bottom of the keel, or the surface of the water, depending on where the transducer is installed on the hull. A transducer emits a high-frequency signal straight down beneath the boat. The signal bounces off the bottom (or off a school of fish for a fish finder) and back up to the transducer. By measuring the time the signal takes to return, the depth sounder calculates the depth of the water. Some models are equipped with alarms to warn distracted skippers of an impending shoal or object.

If a boat's knot meter reads 4 knots and the boat is heading into a 2-knot current, the boat is traveling only 2 knots accross the ocean floor. If the boat turns and runs with the current, the boat will be traveling 6 knots over the floor—

three times faster—yet the knot meter will still read 4 knots.

Another useful device is a wind speed and wind direction indicator, which give a readout in the cockpit from a wind vane and anemometer mounted at the mast head.

The more comforts you can put on a boat, the more pleasurable your sail will be—within limits. I'm not talking about the grand piano that William F. Buckley, Jr., took on his family's trans-Atlantic crossing. What I'm talking about are basic pleasures we take for granted at home, like hot water for showers, refrigeration other than ice blocks, a freezer, stereos and lights.

All these take electricity. On cruises longer than an overnight, a boat's batteries must constantly be recharged, by either starting the engine and motoring for awhile, or starting the generator. Both of these solutions destroy the pleasure of a quiet sail and break the rhythm of the wind.

Wind generators, small windmills with a prop about two feet in diameter, are proving to be an ideal solution for maintaining the batteries. If there's no wind, you'll be thinking about starting the engine anyway. These units are usually mounted on the mizzen mast or on a pole on the stern, away from the sails and rigging. These generators produce only a trickle of electricity, but they can be left on for long periods of time. They will also work during overcast days and through the night.

Solar panels are useful as well but have limitations compared to wind generators. The most obvious limitation is that it must be sunny. They produce even less electricity than wind generators, but need no attention, such as turning on and off.

CHARTS

Navigation charts are an absolute necessity for sailing anywhere along a coast, and in many rivers and larger lakes. Charts are the maps of the waterways, put out by the government, with all the pertinent information for piloting a craft without marked highways or a bottom that you can see. As one navigator said maps show where you can go, charts show where you can't go.

Charts can be purchased at almost any chandlery or marine supply store, for about $6. They are crammed with information.

Charts show the locations of prominent landmarks you can see from the water, such as towers, tanks, steeples, hills, cliffs and lighthouses used to give you bearings.

Charts list water depths usually every 20 to 50 feet, more frequently on smaller scales like in harbors and channels. Shoals and other dangerous areas are well marked. All aids to navigation, such as buoys, lights, markers and lighthouses are marked. There is also helpful information about how far away they can be seen, the frequency patterns of the lights and whistles, and the shapes and colors of the markers themselves, perhaps with any markings or numbering on them.

The top of a chart is always in a northerly direction, but a compass rose is printed on every chart giving a precise marking to line your compass up on. Charts also give latitude and longitude, Loran bearings, distance scales and any other special information the mariner may need, even to the point of listing the composition of harbor bottoms;

such as rocky, hard, or sandy, to assist you in anchoring.

COMPASS

One of the most important items on your boat is the compass. Frequently, even on day sails, you won't be able to see your destination and must steer in the correct direction by watching the compass. You also need a compass in case conditions change. In many areas it's not uncommon for an unexpected fog to roll in and reduce visibility to near-zero. Or, if the wind dies, you could end up sailing home after dark. In such cases, it would be nice to know which direction to steer.

A compass consists of a pair of magnets attached to the underside of a compass card, which spins freely. All magnets, if they can move freely, will automatically line themselves up with the earth's magnetic field. They don't point at the North Pole or even at the magnetic North Pole, but all magnets will always point in the same direction. The difference from that direction to true North will be listed on a navigation chart, and is called magnetic deviation. In order to use a compass accurately, you must know the magnetic deviation for the area in which you are sailing.

Any ferrous metal (steel or iron), electrical charge, or other magnet near a compass will throw the compass off. When steering by compass, it's very important not to have keys, a flashlight or similar objects near the compass. □

BLUE WATER

I hauled the Folkboat out in Hyannis, shaped her up and painted her, and then sailed up to Boston. I was living in Cambridge, in a tiny house not much larger than the Folkboat, and working for the Associated Press. I spent much of that winter in Europe covering the U.S. Ski Team on the World Cup Ski Circuit.

It wasn't all work, however, as I met Betsy Smith, a ski rep living in Stowe, Vermont. Once I got off the ski circuit, I began making the weekly trek up to Stowe. Betsy had grown tired of living in ski towns, however, and announced that she'd like to live in Cambridge.

I had doubts about our living together in my tiny little house in a poor part of town, and sure enough, within two months we bought a house up the coast in Marblehead, a beautiful little town with a magnificent harbor.

I had also guessed that Betsy would soon tire of my little Folkboat. Gradually, we started noticing more and more boats for sale, and began regularly scanning the classified ads in sailing magazines.

"I'll pick you up at 4 o'clock," she told me over the phone at work one day.

"What's up?" I asked.

"We're going to Rhode Island."

I knew immediately that we were going to go look at an 8-Meter we had seen a number of times in several magazines. We had marveled at the lines of the boat, but, seriously, it was 45 feet long and way out of our league. So we had never bothered to call about it.

Sure enough, as soon as I got into Betsy's car she said we were going to look at the 8-Meter.

King Haakon was absolutely stunning. She was massive, all 45 feet of her, but sleek like no other boat I had seen. Her lean, stark white hull carried a 65-foot wooden mast, and, clearly, she was fast.

Stepping onto her fir deck, I knew immediately we would buy her. From her binnacle compass to her beautiful interior, she was exquisite. Built in 1948, she still had original upholstery, of exceptional quality and in quite good shape. Her cabinets were made of beautiful dark mahogany, richly varnished to a dark red, beautifully set off by bright yellow birdseye-maple panels.

She was Norwegian designed and built, with full-length planking with glued seams. In other words, all of her planks were the full length of the boat, cut perfectly to be water-tight without the need for any caulking.

She was originally built for a Norwegian industrialist, and named *Nora II*. In about 1955, an American named Detlov Bronk lost a schooner in a storm in Europe and bought *Nora II* as a replacement. After negotiating the purchase, he wrote the king of Norway, King Haakon, stating he that wanted to rename *Nora II* after the king. Bronk's family told me he received back from the king a hand-written letter on royal stationery stating that it was forbidden to name anything after a living monarch. But, after wishing Bronk good sailing, the king told him almost parenthetically, that if he took the boat to the United States he could go ahead and name it after him. Bronk sailed her to Maine and renamed her. She eventually won Class A in the Marblehead to Halifax race and finished quite well in the Newport-Bermuda Race. Unfortunately, no one in Bronk's family has been able to find the king's letter.

Betsy and I bought *King Haakon* with a few stipulations, one of which was that the seller, Jim McFarlane, would take us sailing a few times to get us acquainted with this monster. When the time came to take possession of the boat, we still hadn't been out sailing and Jim was busy for the next month. What the hell? Why should this be any different than the Hobie Cat? Just dive in.

With a few friends on board that next Saturday, I released the mooring line for the first time and put the engine in gear. I looked long and far to the bow, high up and far to the top of the mast, and choked.

"This thing is huge and is waiting for me to tell it what to do," I thought to myself. "And it will probably do a few things I don't tell it to do."

We didn't get 100 yards into the channel before I stuck the 14,000-pound keel right into a mudbank. Big difference when the keel is six-and-a-half feet deep. With reverse gear and an anchor off the stern, we freed ourselves and continued on.

Sailing down Narragansett Bay under the Newport Bridge, I was overwhelmed by the scale of the world I was moving up to. This boat weighed 23,000 pounds and could glide forever, it seemed. Sailing under huge bridges, passing by ocean freighters and cruise liners, I was awed by how large structures in touch with the ocean could be.

Betsy had the same lack of fear (or common sense) as I did. She suggested, for our first real cruise, that we sail to

Running Aground

One of the absolutes in sailing is running aground. If you sail, then sooner or later, and probably sooner, you will run out of water and be hard aground.

With luck, you will have been ghosting along in no wind, and the bottom will be soft mud. Without luck, you will have been under full sail and hit a very hard, very sharp rock.

With luck, you'll be in fresh water with no currents or tide. Without luck, a six to eight-foot tide has just started running out. Not only are you aground, but your boat is about to lay over on her side for eight to ten hours until the high tide returns and floats you off.

Usually, groundings are nothing to worry about. If the boat is less than 30 feet long, the draft is usually four feet or less. That means you can jump overboard (with shoes on) and push yourself off. With a draft nearing or greater than your height, other measures can be used.

The easiest is to run your engine in reverse. Caution must be used in this procedure because mud is usually kicked up and may be passed over your water intake ports. There is a chance you could clog your cooling water port.

If the engine fails to back you off, throw the anchor as far off the stern as possible. Or row it in the dinghy as far out as practical. You want the angle of pull as low as possible. Have your crew in unison heave away on the line, or wrap it around the largest winch you have.

If your bow is aground, have the entire crew stand as far aft as possible. If the keel is centered on ground, have the entire crew stand and hike out to one side as far as possible. In extreme cases, and this isn't recommended unless you are very experienced with your equipment, it's possible to tie the anchor to a halyard and row the anchor out to the side a good distance. By taking in the halyard against the anchor, the boat heels itself clear of the grounding. Care must be taken once free not to damage the mast or the halyard or pop the halyard sideways out of the masttop sheave. The last alternative is to hail a power vessel for a tow.

If all methods fail and the tide is draining, you'll have to pre-pare your boat to lay over on its side until the next high tide, a maximum of 12 hours later. Place flotation cushions or a sailbag between the hull and the point it touches on the ground to prevent scraping. If the water is calm, you'll be OK. In rough water, you could have serious trouble.

In nearly every case, you'll float off eventually, usually with the greatest damage not to the boat, but to your pride.

Nantucket, a long, two-day trip from our mooring. I agreed, seeing how it was mid-September and I wanted to make a few good trips on our new boat before the season ended.

So, with another couple, who had never been on a sailboat before, we shoved off on a Saturday morning. We anchored the first night in the lee of Penikese Island, a tiny speck of an island that had been used as a leper colony earlier this century.

Up early the next morning, the weather was clear, with good winds to carry us all day through Vineyard Sound and out to Nantucket, where I planned to make my heralded return on this big beautiful yacht.

Minor problems plagued us each time we opened a drawer, or pulled out a different sail. We blew out the clew of one sail, tore the handles off a few drawers, and couldn't get the head to work properly.

We arrived off Nantucket at dusk. About a mile out, I doused the sails and started the engine. It was dark as we reached the two rock jetties forming the channel into Nantucket Harbor. I was happy to be returning to this charming little place, especially on such a grand boat.

Suddenly the engine coughed, coughed again and died. Right there in the middle of the channel. Soon the ferry would be entering the channel, it was dark and we were stopped right in the middle.

Terrified, I dove into the engine compartment. For some reason, I remembered from way back somewhere that when a diesel engine runs out of fuel, the fuel lines must have the air bled out of them. It's amazing what comes to you when you need it. I don't have a clue where I learned that, but it was true. I had forgotten to turn on the fuel valve and the engine had run dry. I turned on the valve, but there was still a problem: I didn't have a clue how to bleed the fuel lines.

Sure enough, the ferry appeared in the channel and slowed to a crawl. The crackle came over the radio to the vessel blocking the entrance to Nantucket. I ran up to the cockpit, waved a flashlight at the ferry's wheelhouse, and told Paul to take the tiller. Then I radioed the ferry that we were without power. A Coast Guard boat followed the ferry past us. So I radioed the Coast Guard cutter and told him my situation.

He went into reverse, turned on enough deck lights to light up Fenway Park and began giving me instructions to raft up to him. They wanted all of us in life jackets. The cutter was gigantic, with massive ear-splitting exhaust pipes, and about 15 men on deck holding lines to toss down to us.

I was in a dither, overwhelmed. Hell, the size of my boat had me in awe. Now we were rafting up alongside a ship three times the size of mine, and all in a narrow channel.

We lashed ourselves tight, the Coast Guard skipper masterfully moved us into the harbor and gently coaxed my boat and his into the dock. The crew walked our lines back off their stern and tied us to the dock. I thanked them profusely and they casually said they'd stop by tomorrow and show me how to bleed the air lines. Real professionals.

By now, I was totally drained. I needed a beer. As I stumbled below exhausted, there were Betsy and Pam, with a full spread of cheese, pâté, and crackers out on the table. They were in their life jackets, howling at each others' jokes, having a wonderful time, oblivious to all that was going on topside. They thought it had been a grand adventure and were glad to be in Nantucket.

King Haakon triggered an exponential growth in my sailing experiences. I entered the world of "big boats" and sailing longer distances with more people. This usually entailed some bigger risks, too. Soon, I was asked to crew on some of the old wooden 12-Meters.

Sailing big boats involves knowledge and skill that comes only from experience. There's nothing mysterious about it, but it's not something you can read in a "how-to" book. Gaining that experience can put you in some interesting, if not compromising, positions.

Jack and Anna Vultee owned a 25-footer on Cape Cod and were itching to sail on a bigger boat. So they joined us one weekend for a run 20 miles out to Block Island.

As we raised the sails, the wind backed around to our stern and I suggested we put up the spinnaker. Running before the wind is the most comfortable point of sail; the wind and the seas are going in the same direction as the boat, the boat remains level and dry, and if the sun is out, it's heaven.

The spinnaker on *King Haakon*, although made of very lightweight nylon, was an enormous, powerful sail that measured 72 feet along the sides, almost large enough to cover a small house. The trick in setting a spinnaker is to get it up and open. Then it's easy to control.

As Jack and I started pulling the spinnaker up, fluky winds caused it to oscillate, and finally wrap itself around the headstay. I had Betsy take the halyard, the line that pulls the sail up, while I went forward on the bow to help Jack untangle the sail.

Jack and I leaned well out over the bow, trying to free the sail. We were moving at about eight or nine knots through the water. The movement of the boat was not abrupt, but it wasn't steady, and balance was difficult while leaning out muscling such a large sail. Looking straight down, we could see blue water with the white bow wave rolling five feet under us.

I was stretched out and straining when suddenly the sail started to go up. I yelled back to Betsy not to raise it yet. She said she didn't do anything. A few seconds later, the sail went higher up the headstay, causing me to lean even farther out.

"Betsy, don't raise the sail yet, dammit," I yelled forward, not being able to turn around.

"I'm not doing anything, Mike, the wind is doing it," she said.

It was not going right, and both Jack and I were getting very tired straining so hard. We were very close to getting the problem solved when all of a sudden the sail went five feet higher. Both of us nearly fell overboard, but we managed to grab the bow rail on the way over.

"Goddammit, Betsy," I screamed as I climbed back on deck, "I told you not to raise the sail!" Furious, I looked back only to see Betsy in midair, desperately clinging to the rope. The wind had pulled the sail up and out, lifting Betsy clean off the deck.

Needless to say, I felt like a mole, and ran back and lifted her down. She had torn the skin on her palms, afraid to let go. It was a long time before she forgave me.

Sailing is always full of things you could never possibly expect.

Walter Nickerson and I threw together a great sailing trip one fall, out to Block Island for the night, then on down to Essex, Connecticut. We were on Block Island Sound, headed northwest for the passage between Long Island, New York, and Fisher's Island, New York. The wind was perfect—10 to 15 knots out of the southeast—so we flew the big blue and yellow spinnaker. I checked the chart for the location of a buoy marking the western side of the passage—Little Gull shoal just east of Long Island. I spotted the buoy several miles off the port bow.

We opened some Cokes and, in sailing parlance, "started the lamp swinging" by telling sea stories. Always some truths, always some lies, and everything exaggerated. Several stories and a lot of laughs later, I glanced toward the buoy, and couldn't find it. We had been keeping it in the 10-o'clock to 11-o'clock position, and Walter spotted it at 1 o'clock. So I turned the boat to starboard, until the buoy was repositioned where we needed it, trimmed the sails and continued on with the stories.

A short while later, I was offcourse again, having drifted to port again. This was strange and didn't feel right, because the wind hadn't been changing and the sun was wrong. Anyway, based on the buoy, I swung the boat farther to starboard, trimmed the sails again and kept sailing.

About five minutes later, Walter, who loves to hound me about being a lousy sailor (relative to him), yelled that

12-Meter Boats

In Newport, Rhode Island, there is a strong movement to bring back the grand old days of America's Cup racing in wooden yachts. Started nearly fifteen years ago by Robert Tiedemann, Seascope Systems now offers eight 12-Meter America's Cup boats for charter, along with two classic 130-foot J-Boats—with masts taller than 12-story buildings.

These boats have all been restored to their original grandeur and offer the public access to the golden age of sailboat racing when money virtually was no object. The boats can be chartered individually or as a fleet for informal match-racing against each other in America's Cup style.

The two J-Boats, Shamrock V and Endeavour, are famous old America's Cup racers from the 1930s, the era when Sir Thomas Lipton spent a large part of his tea fortune unsuccessfully attempting to wrest the America's Cup from Cornelius Vanderbilt and his sailing cronies. Elizabeth Meyers recently spent more than $10 million restoring Endeavour to original condition, and it is a sight to see, as well as to sail on. Shamrock was also freshly restored before being donated to the Museum of Yachting in Newport.

Contact: Seascope Systems, Box 119, Newport, Rhode Island 02840; tel.: 401/847-5007.

I had drifted off course—couldn't I drive this thing correctly? I knew something was wrong and I knew that it was not my fault. Taking the binoculars, I looked out at the buoy, only to see white water breaking around it. I checked the chart. Something was wrong because Little Gull buoy was in 75 feet of water.

Walter, now on the bow with the binoculars, was laughing hysterically. He had figured it out. This one would be good. He handed me the binoculars and told me to just watch the buoy for a few seconds. Sure as hell, it was the tower of a submarine cruising slowly eastward across the passage. I had been altering course, keeping the boat aimed at the sub. Little Gull buoy by now was about five miles to the west.

In the days prior to the 1986 tax law revisions, charter boat companies put together a terrific package for people who (A) loved to sail and (B) were paying a high proportion of their income to the tax man.

The charter company would buy a boat for you with your down payment, charter it out in the Caribbean, and maintain it. If the company was good, they would cover the boat's expenses out of the charter fees and you would break even. For no more than the initial down payment, you would get to sail the boat for a month or six weeks every year AND you would get to write the boat off as depreciation on your tax returns. This could offset a sizeable amount of income for some people as well as give them use of a boat with no maintenance worries.

Dozens and dozens of charter companies set up in the

Caribbean, particularly in the Virgin Islands, using this structure. Some made money, many lost, but the net result was that chartering boomed, and suddenly there were all kinds of charter boats that had to be sailed down to the Caribbean. For me and my friends, it was a bonanza: they'd pay us to sail 'em down, well stocked with food and booze, then give us plane tickets home—paid vacations!

The best and the worst of these jobs came on a two-week delivery from Ft. Lauderdale to St. Thomas, U.S. Virgin Islands. The boat was a 44-foot sloop, French designed and built in Belgium. It was owned by a business-man who, along with the boat, had best remain nameless.

The boat was shipped over from Belgium on the deck of a freighter to Ft. Lauderdale, where the mast was stepped and rigged. Five of us flew down from Boston, and a sixth flew in from Atlanta. The three women—Sue, Sally and Paula—had very little sailing experience. The two other guys, Jamie and Foggy (helluva name for a sailor, though, even more improbable was his last name, Wing, since he was a pilot for Air New England), had some experience. I was the only one with any offshore experience, and by default, I became skipper.

The boat was well-appointed both on deck and down below. It had three private cabins, a beautiful main salon, great galley and very efficient nav station. Its new diesel was adequately powerful, complete with a generator for hot water, freezer, tape deck, etc. The headsail had roller furling and the main was a stowaway. Translated, the genoa furled around the headstay, while the mainsail furled around a cable inside the mast. Both furling lines could be operated from the cockpit, thus eliminating the need to go forward and drop the sails during a storm. The boat was goldplated, as they say, and we were excited about this sail.

After three days of outfitting the boat, renting survival gear and stocking up on food and water, and charts, and checking the electronics, we were ready. I even bought a bushel of oranges and another of grapefruits, just so scurvy wouldn't set in.

We were one of nine boats to be delivered at the same time. The eight other skippers decided to take the scenic route down through all the islands, twisting and turning, dodging coral reefs, staying close to shore. We decided to sail due east right through the Bahamas to the outside and carve a big, wide arc all the way down to St. Thomas, a distance of about 1,300 miles.

We were the first boat ready to go and decided not to wait. After a big send-off dinner, we left the dock at midnight to catch a fair tide.

We weren't out of the channel before we found a problem with the freshwater system—we couldn't pump up drinking water from one of the tanks. But we figured we could fix it underway, so we continued sailing. With pitch darkness ahead and the lighted skyline of Ft. Lauderdale growing dim behind us, we ran a radio check, which no one answered. After numerous attempts, we realized that the radio wasn't working properly; now we had to turn back.

Back in Ft. Lauderdale we replaced some fittings in the water tank and found that the radio antenna wasn't hooked up. It would work at the dock because there the

antenna wasn't needed. We fixed that and shoved off again, this time at 9 A.M., into a foul tide.

We quickly settled into our routines of watches, cooking, reading and sunning. I figured it would take a few days before everyone was fairly comfortable, so any complaints or problems would work themselves out in due time.

We didn't have any electronic navigation gear on board, just a compass and a sextant, which Foggy was intent on learning. He did a pretty good job keeping track of our course, as long as he could find the sun. Once, a Coast Guard plane came down about 100 feet off the water and circled us, looking for drug boats, I guess. I radioed him for a fix on our location, and he casually radioed back, "Roger, skipper. I'll be back to you in a few minutes," and flew off to the horizon. He came back four minutes later with our exact location, to within 25 feet. I was amazed at how a plane passing by could pinpoint us that accurately that quickly. Foggy, incidentally, had us within a few miles, which was impressive for a sextant.

On the fourth day out, the sun vanished. The wind started to whip up, the freshwater tank developed a leak and we needed to catch our breath. So we decided that night to put in to land. The closest landfall was a group of some little islands just south of the Bahamas, the Turks and Caicos Islands. Jamie knew of them because of some biologist friends doing research there. So we figured we would rest for a day and top off the fresh water.

We altered course in the night and sailed well into the morning before we finally sighted land. By now, the wind was really howling, the seas were beginning to build and I was glad we were getting out of it. We sailed up to a small fishing boat and asked where the channel was between Grand Turk Island and South Caicos. Fishermen love it when expensive yachts ask them for directions. They invariably stare at you in total silence for about ten minutes before saying anything. This one didn't say a word. He just pointed down a channel and kept working, hauling his net by hand.

We sailed down the channel about three miles, then turned into a large harbor lined with the hulks of four sunken fishing boats barely sticking up out of the water. In true island fashion, the boats sank and the owners just left them there, right in the harbor. There were three docks, a tiny boat yard for fishing boats, about 20 houses and a small hotel with a bar. We were the only sailboat, and the only tourists. We sensed some adventure, but had no idea it would be a step back in time, right out of Rod Serling's "Twilight Zone."

An adorable little kid named Fever, who was probably about 12, met us as we came ashore. He told us about the hotel and walked us down to immigration. After checking with the officer, who I think was also the school teacher, the fire department, and a part-time fisherman, we walked over to the hotel for some information on fresh water, food, laundry, etc. On the way over, Fever told us everyone on the island had a nickname, his because he was so sick as a child.

The desk clerk, a kind man with one eye askew, named Crabeye, told us everything we needed to know. We walked into the bar and ordered six simple drinks, which took the lady 35 minutes to make. No problem, mon. We were on island time.

Every island has one person who can get you anything, who knows everyone you need to meet, johnny-on-the-spot, for a price. While we were in the bar, we found, or were found by, the great expeditor of South Caicos Island—Deuce. Deuce had two teeth, hence his name.

Deuce had more energy than any two men. His goal in life was to get to the States and become a disc jockey. To prepare for this, once a week, on Saturday mornings, he would take his little boat over to Grand Turk Island, where NASA has a missile tracking station and a huge communications setup. Apparently, the station had a small radio station with a turntable. Deuce was allowed to play records and chat over the radio for a couple of hours every Saturday morning.

Our biggest concern was finding fresh water, which was in short supply on South Caicos. The chain of islands was formed by coral, with no dirt and thus no ground water. The islanders collected rain water for all their water needs. Every downspout from every roof ran into a cistern.

We arranged, through Deuce, to buy some water at one of the docks. Deuce introduced us to Friday, a waterfront kingpin who just happened to be the fisher-man who had given us directions into the channel the day before.

A crowd of about 15 fishermen formed around us, purely out of curiosity and an excuse not to work. Friday, making sure we recognized his position at the top of the pecking order, said he could easily help us, then turned and barked at someone to "go find White Man Slave."

The crowd (which was entirely black) sensed our uneasiness and quietly smiled to each other, starting to

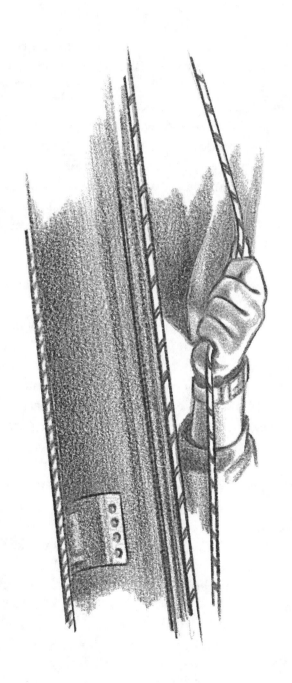

enjoy this one. We three white boys quickly glanced at each other, and decided that if something was happening there was nothing we could do about it, so we might as well play along.

Soon a slightly built white man, half asleep with big glasses on the end of his nose, arrived wearing a zipped-up fatigue coat and a woolen watch cap. It was 80 degrees. Friday told him to get us some water and he left, dutifully, without a word. We learned that he had been here in the military, had apparently fried his brains on drugs of some kind and returned after he was discharged. He lived in Friday's basement, was basically unable to work and was taken care of by all the islanders. Only in jest was he in servitude, but the fishermen loved the idea of it.

White Man Slave returned, straining under the weight of two five-gallon buckets filled with water. We told Friday that we needed about 150 gallons, and that White Man Slave would take all day at this rate. Friday immediately sent Fever to go fetch Whiskey, and tell him to have Faithful Jack bring some water. We didn't ask.

About 30 minutes later, as we began to relax and enjoy some of the fishermen's jokes, everyone pointed down the road. An old, gray-haired man walked his mule toward us. The mule was hitched to a two-wheeled cart, carrying a 55-gallon drum of water.

Whiskey walked his mule right up to the edge of the dock and ordered, "Whoa, Faithful Jack. Turn around now."

Faithful Jack, a droopy-eyed mule who had to be older than Whiskey, faithfully turned around the cart and, on command, backed the cart up onto the dock. Whiskey started to siphon water out of the drum and we began a very efficient brigade of buckets of water to the boat. No problem, mon.

It wasn't until we had the tanks full that Friday said we should treat the water, something we had never even thought about. We looked into the tanks, only to see a number of bugs in it, along with some things we couldn't identify. We poured a small amount of bleach into each tank and, once we got used to the slight taste, had no problem.

That afternoon, Fever took us around town on a guided walking tour. As we passed the police station, he glanced up in surprise and then picked up the pace considerably, glancing back at the police station about every fifth step, muttering something about school. Finally a policeman came running out of the station and jumped into a Land Rover. Fever bolted between two houses, the policeman went roaring around the corner in hot pursuit and we never saw either again.

The next day we decided to get underway, only to be turned back by huge waves and a roaring wind just outside the channel. We voted to give the storm one more night to blow over, and sailed back into the protected harbor for the night. That evening, we took our inflatable dinghy across the channel to Grand Turk Island, crawled over the fence of the missile tracking station, and met some of the Americans working there. We used their showers, then went to the equivalent of the officer's club for hamburgers, beers, and stories.

The base was the first in a line of tracking stations around the world that would pick up rockets launched at Cape Canaveral. Because of its massive radar installation, it was also used by the U.S. government to monitor suspected drug traffic flying up from Columbia. Several of the operators there told us that the airstrip at South Caicos was the last safe refueling stop for the drug-laden planes on their way into Florida. This was somewhat confirmed by the owner of the charter company for whom we were delivering the boat. I telephoned to let him know our location and progress, and he virtually flipped out, screaming at me to get away from the Turks and Caicos, that it was a notorious haven for pirates looking to shanghai delivery boats and press them into drug service.

I suspected that the myth was larger than the reality, since we hadn't seen another American except at the radar base. We had a small pistol on board in case we met pirates along the delivery route, but we didn't bother to take it out. There just wasn't any perceived threat.

The next day, we shoved off again. This time the waves were even larger and the wind stronger. I wanted to turn around, but by now everyone had decided we were too far behind in our schedule and that we should venture out into it. A bad mistake.

Without realizing it, we found ourselves in a stationary front—a large, angry storm slowly moving southeast at 5 knots. Our course, as well, was southeast, and we were managing about 5 knots. When we sailed out of the channel, we were in the middle of the storm. We were to spend the next five days in 40-knot winds and 15-foot seas.

Life on board quickly turned very hard. We didn't take the seas head on, but on the port bow, which helped the

Safety

The key to good sailing is to be prepared for any situation, and to expect the unexpected. Trouble is bound to appear, and having the proper safety equipment on board will minimize the consequences.

On daysailers, capsizes are expected, and most boats are designed to be righted by a single person. Still, you'll want some safety equipment, such as a life jacket for each person, a whistle or horn for hailing help, a hand-held compass for fog or nighttime, and a paddle for rowing. Some sailors secure rigid foam under the bow and stern to prevent the boat from sinking.

Larger, farther-ranging boats require more safety equipment. On offshore cruising boats, the worst fear for any skipper is having someone fall overboard at night. In any kind of sea, it's virtually impossible to spot a head among the crest of waves. It's also virtually impossible to steer a perfect circle and come back on the same spot where the person fell overboard.

For starters, all crew members at night or in bad storms should be harnessed to the boat, with stout harnesses made of canvas webbing securely attached to cable lifelines. A life vest is worn over the safety harness.

If someone does go over, you need safety equipment that can readily be thrown into the water. Near the stern should be two horseshoe life preservers, easily removed and thrown. A swimmer can enter these without ducking his or her head under water. The horseshoes should have tethered strobe lights that activate once in the water, and a whistle. A tall man-overboard pole, with an automatic strobe light, should be attached to the backstay, ready to be thrown into the water. This gives the skipper a mark to steer toward, and the person overboard something to swim to.

On long voyages, it is imperative to prepare for the possibility of the boat sinking. A life raft large enough to accommodate everyone should be properly installed on deck. Minimum equipment should include rations, water, a canopy to escape the sun, flares and an EPIRB, an emergency radio transmitter that sends a distress signal to channels monitored by ships and airplanes. Solar-powered desalinization units for purifying salt water are becoming more popular and cheaper in price. The better life rafts are equipped with a plethora of odds and ends, such as mirrors for signaling, fish hooks, knives, first-aid kids, salt and vitamin tablets, and sunscreen.

motion considerably and kept us from slamming. But still it was up the face of a wave, over and down the back, then up the next and down its back. The boat heeled steadily at about 20 degrees. Rain was intermittent, salt-water sprayed constantly off the bow with every wave. Full foulweather gear, buttoned around the face, was the rule. Even then the salt got into our eyes and caked on our lashes.

How quickly the weather can dampen a crew's spirit. If you weren't on watch, it was too wet and nasty to stay topside. Down below, moving around was too hard, so most of the crew just went to their bunks when not on watch. It was impossible to dry out, everything leaked including the decks. Once, looking for some tweezers, I opened the drawer in my cabin dresser only to find my passport, wallet and other papers floating in a mixture of sea water and diesel fuel that had leaked from some jerry cans in the cockpit. Organized meals also stopped and people just munched on whatever they could find.

Occasionally the wind would change direction or pick up so strongly that we would have to furl the sails and motor. I wasn't aware of how much we had been motor-ing until the engine died one night. We had completely drained one of the fuel tanks and sent an airlock into the fuel line that killed the engine.

Slamming around in the seas, I felt nearly defeated. We switched to the other fuel tank, but once a diesel engine runs out of fuel, the fuel line must be bled of air before the engine will start. The engine was accessible but diffi-cult to reach, even at the dock. The fuel line was even harder to reach.

We were having trouble just moving around in the cabin, fighting off seasickness and irritability. However, Foggy, through a superhuman effort, managed to squeeze his body upside down alongside the engine and concentrate long enough to uncouple the fuel line fitting. He yelled to crank the engine, which I did. Fuel spilled into his face, bilge water sloshed around, but he managed to bleed the line into a pan, then reconnect the fitting and tighten it. The engine fired right up. I shall never forget Foggy's raw courage on that night.

Jamie and Sally took the next watch while the rest of us slept. Sue was either asleep or playing possum well. I tossed and turned, worrying about the storm and the boat and the crew.

Water started leaking into the anchor compartment forward in the bow. The leak was coming from a crack in the deck, which I didn't think was new, nor did I think it was structurally important. I figured someone had dropped the anchor, or it had slammed up in one of the seas. But as much as I told myself it wasn't significant, I couldn't stop thinking about it.

I also knew that we didn't have that much fuel left in the other tank, and the jerry cans of fuel in the cockpit had become contaminated with seawater. We had to sail more and forget about the engine and generator.

Soon, the call came for Sue and me to take our watch. Jamie said the wind was blowing a steady 40 knots but that the seas were building and becoming confused. He had slammed the bow into the seas a number of times, so I knew it was getting rougher.

Sue and I climbed into our wet foulweather gear and

came on deck. We lashed ourselves in with the safety harnesses and I took the 5-foot diameter wheel. In the darkness, it was nearly impossible to see the waves, much less steer through them.

About ten minutes into our watch, I heard an ominous sound, like a wave breaking. Only it wasn't where it should be. I jumped around to the left and looked up to see a freak wave coming at us directly on our beam, the top of it breaking nearly 20 feet up, near the spreaders on the mast.

I yelled and lurched the wheel to port, trying desperately to get the bow pointed into the wave. Too late. The wave picked us up and rolled us over nearly 90 degrees, with the mast almost parallel to the water. Foaming water came crashing over the cockpit, knocking Sue through the lifelines and into the sea. I managed to hang onto the wheel, with my legs hanging through the lifelines.

As quickly as it hit us, the wave continued on its way and the boat righted itself. I immediately ran to the side and pulled Sue, who luckily wasn't hurt, back on board. Down below, everyone had been sleeping on the starboard side so they weren't thrown but a few feet when we rolled. The cabin was a mess, with gear thrown everywhere. Luckily, Jamie had closed the companionway hatch when he went down below. Still, with the vertical doorway open, hundreds of gallons of water had crashed into the cabin. Cushions were everywhere, books, tapes, clothes—everything was a mess.

No one was hurt and a quick inspection showed nothing was lost overboard. We found that a one-half-inch thick plywood teak bulkhead between the galley and the

main salon had sheared in half. We were unable to find any other structural problems with the boat, but the bulkhead really bothered me. The entire hull must have contorted for that plywood to break. The mast and rigging appeared fine, the sails were OK, so we were basically just bruised. And scared.

Just after dawn, we went to reef the jib in some more when the shackle on the jib halyard broke. The halyard stayed up near the masthead, and the jib slid down the forestay. The only possible way of fixing it was to climb the mast, which was out of the question in these seas. The boat sailed very poorly under the main alone. The only choice was to motor the rest of the way. However, a quick check of the remaining fuel tank showed we had three gallons left—maximum. Now we were stuck.

I was so tired and irritable, so sick of the situation, that I went to the radio and called the Coast Guard. I said we were disabled and that we needed a tow. We were approximately 90 miles off the coast of Puerto Rico.

"Roger, skipper," came the reply. "Is your situation life-threatening?"

"No, we're in no danger of sinking. We do not have a life-threatening situation."

"Roger, skipper. Be advised that due to the severity of the storm we're unable to provide assistance to any vessel that is not in a life-threatening situation. We have everything out right now, with several boats going down."

So what are we supposed to do? Bob around out here? Then the Coast Guard came back.

"Roger, skipper. If we were to supply you with fuel, could you make it into port on your own power?"

"Affirmative."

"Give us your exact location and we will send a helicopter out to you as soon as we can."

I told him we were about 90 miles out, which he said wasn't good enough. I said it was the best we could do. He said we'd have to do better. So I said we would hope for a freighter or cruise ship to come by and tell us where we were.

Just as I cleared off the air, the captain of a container ship radioed and asked if that was us off his port bow. Foggy ran to the companionway, and through the spray and rain could see a massive ship plowing through the seas. We flashed our emergency masthead strobe light on, which he identified. Then he gave us our exact location.

The Coast Guard had monitored our transmissions and said they would have a helicopter out to us by late afternoon. Any help was to be appreciated, even if we had to wait all day.

We tried sailing under the mainsail alone, but it was worthless and more aggravating than helpful. So we just rested and cleaned up the boat.

Around 4 P.M., the Coast Guard radioed that a helicopter was leaving San Juan with six cans of fuel on board. The sky was beginning to clear, with low lying clouds letting some sun through. Soon, a giant rescue helicopter was churning through the clouds toward us, two huge vortexes of clouds swirling down and away from his rotor. What a great sight.

As he hovered over us about 100 feet up, the pilot radioed that he was lowering a sandbag on a line to us, which we were to grab. The line would be attached to a

116

stretcher carrying the cans of fuel and we should use the line to pull it in.

After much flailing around, grabbing the air and missing the sand bag, it suddenly came rocketing toward me and hit me in the chest. I grabbed it and now we had a link to the chopper.

Three guys with white helmets pushed a life-saving stretcher out the side door of the chopper and lowered it down. The pilot warned us not to touch the stretcher or the cable before it hit the rigging. As soon as the stretcher got within a few feet of the backstay, a brilliant white electric arc jumped across. The pilot said that was the static electricity built up in the helicopter. Now it would be safe to touch.

The stretcher with six cans of fuel weighed so much that we couldn't hang on to it. There must have been 300 pounds, swinging on a 100-foot pendulum. The helicopter was buffeting 40-knot winds and we were bobbing on 12-foot seas. We would get the stretcher near the boat and either the helicopter or the boat would move and the polypropylene line would go zinging through my hands. Again and again we tried with no luck. Finally, against the pilot's instructions, I tied the line to a winch on the mast and tried to hold it. The line parted. Up went the stretcher into the helicopter, down came another sandbag with a new line and we started all over again.

We broke three lines when finally the pilot said they had no more gear, they'd have to return in about an hour.

On the second trip out, I suggested putting just one can at a time in the stretcher. That seemed to work better, and we finally landed it on the deck. I dove into the

Seasickness

Seasickness can dampen a daysail and turn a long passage into unmitigated misery.

Motion sickness is believed to be caused by an overabundance of stimuli, which throws your eyes and ears out of sync. Your eyes tell your brain how your body is moving, but the motion sensors in your inner ear, unable to keep up with the pitching, rolling, and yawing, send different signals.

Even experts can become seasick, but the novice is more susceptible to motion sickness. Experienced sailers' bodies adjust over time to the ocean environment, and experts know more about how to deal with mal de mer. *Supposedly the only true cure for seasickness is staying ashore, but the remedies on board fall roughly into three categories—internal, external and behavioral.*

The internal remedies are chemical. Dramamine and Bonine are among the most popular over-the-counter motion sickness drugs. Pamine and Antivert are prescription drugs. Check with your physician before taking any kind of motion-sickness medicine. Common side effects of most pills are dryness of the mouth and drowsiness. You also have to plan ahead and take the pills before you begin your trip because it's usually too late to take a pill once you feel sick.

One of the most revolutionary advances in the battle against seasickness has been the development of external patches. Patches affixed behind the ear or to one's wrist can drastically reduce motion sickness. Ear patches slowly release medicine through the skin into the bloodstream. The advantages of ear patches are long-lasting duration (up to three days) although, as with pills, many users experience dryness of the mouth or feel drowsy. Bands attached on the wrist can reduce nausea through acupressure. Pressure points on the body relate to different maladies, and the bands maintain pressure on points that affect seasickness.

On the behavioral front, several common-sense activities and dietary adjustments can mitigate motion sickness. One of the best things you can do is close your eyes—it also helps to lie down, preferably on deck. Stay aft or amidships, where motion is less severe. If you need to keep your eyes open, concentrating your vision on the horizon can give your eyes a stable reference point.

Certain foods also reduce the effects of motion sickness. Ginger reduces nausea, and ginger ale or ginger snaps can quiet your stomach.

There are no surefire cures for seasickness. If it happens to you, remember—it will be over.

stretcher to untie the can, the boat went down a wave, the helicopter went up, and now I was in the stretcher, five feet off the deck. We came back down and I jumped out with the can. Then we suggested no stretcher, just the cans, which they tried.

The cans slamed and wraped around the rigging. It was a Chinese fire drill. Finally, after being assured that the lids were waterproof, I told the chopper to just lower the cans into the water next to the boat and we would pull them on board. That worked fine. We finally got six five-gallon cans on board. The chopper wished us well and departed. We were so tired we could barely wave goodbye. They had been real pros, though, and we thanked them on the radio for a fine job.

Soon, we were in for another fire drill. The fuel tank fitting in the deck was about two inches in diameter. We had a tiny funnel, the jerry cans had big wide mouths about four inches in diameter, and we were still in large seas that occasionally came on deck. Plus it was dark now. We knew this would never work.

Down below in the main salon, we pulled the cush-ions away from a fuel tank and exposed a large inspection plate on the tank, about a foot in diameter, which we removed. Now all we had to do was pour the cans into this big hole.

The floor of the cabin was soaking wet. As soon as I unscrewed the lid of the first one, some diesel fuel sloshed out, which, mixed with the water, turned the floor into a skating rink. Finally, Jamie braced himself on the bunk and grabbed Foggy from behind, who braced himself against the table and grabbed me from behind. I picked up the forty-pound can, the bow lifted up on a wave and the three of us went sliding back into the galley.

Of the six cans totaling thirty gallons, we probably got twenty gallons into the tank. Enough to get to San Juan. We fired the engine up, cleaned up the best we could and headed for land.

We arrived in old San Juan, Puerto Rico, at dawn, and by 8 A.M. were tied up at the Customs dock, totally bedraggled, exhausted and filthy.

As soon as Foggy secured the dock lines, he stepped over a cable into the parking lot of the Customs house. A freshly scrubbed secretary, on her way to work, saw this monster in full foul weather gear coming toward her and promptly walked in the other direction. Foggy knelt down and kissed the pavement. He would never leave land again, at least not on this boat.

The Coast Guard came on board, as is usual, and inspected us. They laughed at the amount of their gear we had from the airlift the night before. But they approved us and wished us well.

The harbor was packed with boats waiting the storm out. Just as we tied onto a mooring, a Coast Guard cutter towed in the 115-foot yawl *Sayonara,* which had become disabled in the storm. We felt good that at least we had made it under our own power.

San Juan was it, though; we never made it to St. Thomas. The boat was basically unseaworthy. The owner of the charter company sent over a representative from Hood, the manufacturer of the roller furling system that failed. We gave the rep a two-page list of problems with the boat, caught a cab to the airport, and flew home.

WORLD OF SAILING
Shipping Hazards

In theory, sailboats always have the right-of-way over power-boats. In reality on the open ocean, however, huge tankers and freighters might not agree.

Sterling Hayden, the actor/sailor and author of *Wanderer*, stated it succinctly: "Tonnage has the right of way."

Every sailor fears entering the shipping lanes, particularly at night, and being run over. The sheer size of ocean vessels dictates that the rules are different. You might say that an 80-foot yacht is certainly nothing to be ignored. But freighters and tankers, particularly the supertankers, can be more than 10 times that length, with their steel bows higher than the yacht's mast.

Sailing vessels are no match for these behemoths. Even the fishing draggers, as large as 130 feet, sometimes fall victim to a fast-moving freighter on autopilot.

Stories abound of freighters not picking up sailing vessels on their radar. At times, they are on autopilot, perhaps with the helmsman down below getting a cup of coffee. On long passages, the helmsman can simply have a lapse of attention and fail to watch his radar scope.

If there is a collision, many of the ships are so large that the crew cannot even feel the collision, nor hear it if the wind is blowing. Ideally, a collision alarm would alert the helmsman. No one can ever stake their life on ideal conditions, though, especially electronics in a marine environment.

Can't the sailboat avoid the collisions, you ask? In most

cases, yes. But sailing helmsmen also have lapses of attention.

On my first yacht delivery, as we neared the North Carolina coast I was wide awake, alert and aware of my surroundings—but intent on getting the boat to surf down a following sea, and focused on the lighthouse ahead of us, dreaming only of seeing my friends on shore.

It was only half an hour since I had last scanned the horizons. Off the port quarter was a monstrous freighter plowing through the seas on a collision course with me. I was sailing at about 6 knots; I estimated his speed between 20 and 25 knots. Had we both kept our course, we would have collided in a few minutes.

I altered course to starboard and avoided the collision. He never changed his direction one degree. Perhaps he saw me, perhaps he didn't. I'll never know. The water crashing off his bow was enough to bury our boat. His bow would have sent us down in less than a minute.

Another danger is tugboats towing barges, a very common method of coastal shipping. Once underway out of the harbor, the tugboats pay out a towline nearly one-quarter of a mile long. At night, tugboats exhibit a certain combination of running lights when they have a barge under tow.

All mariners are supposed to know these light formations. However, many don't. The distance between the tug and the barge is so great that it's hard to mentally connect the two. And it's impossible to see the steel cable between them. Nearly every sailor I know has a story about a sailboat crossing the wake of a tugboat, never expecting a moving cable in the water directly ahead. Sailboats have been sliced by the cable, or trapped with their keel on it and crushed by the oncoming barge.

A third very real concern are submarines. There is nothing that the prudent sailor can do to prevent a collision with a submarine.

Submarines are equipped with ultrasensitive listening devices that enable them to identify almost any object in the water. Despite their sophisticated sonar gear, however, submarines collide with small recreational and commercial vessels all over the world.

I once went out on a fishing dragger off the south shore of Long Island, New York. We would set the net to drag the bottom of the seabed several hundred feet behind us, and would tow the net for two hours at a time, during which we would eat and sometimes nap. During one of these tows, the skipper told me about a time he and his brother set the net, put the boat on automatic pilot and went to bed.

A while later, the skipper was thrown violently out of his bunk. He ran to the helm, but couldn't figure out what was wrong. Suddenly, he realized the dragger was going backward. He ran out and cut his net cables. He had an identification tag on the net. Two weeks later, he received a card from the navy's submarine base in New London, Connecticut, that one of their subs had surfaced with his net draped around the bow. The navy told him he could drive over and pick up his net.

He was lucky. Others have not fared as well. In June, 1989, *U.S.S. Houston*, a nuclear-powered, fast-attack submarine, caught the towing cable of a tugboat towing two barges of crushed rock from Santa Catalina Island to Long Beach. The tugboat was dragged under by the 360-foot submarine, and sank in less than 40 seconds. The pilot, who was below deck checking on the engine, drowned. The captain and a crewmember swam to safety on the barges.

The captain said he got out of the tugboat no more than 35 or 40 seconds after he woke up, and the tug was already 20 feet under water.

The submarine had been in the Los Angeles area for the filming of *The Hunt for Red October,* a movie about a defecting Soviet submarine captain. The U.S. Navy's investigation determined that the submarine skipper had identified the tugboat, but did not see the 1,000-foot long towing cable or the barges being towed.

Two nights later, the same submarine sliced through fishing nets being towed by a 33-foot boat. The fisherman said he saw the sub's periscope coming toward his nets. He grabbed a knife and cut the lines as soon as the sub snagged the nets. He said he would have been dragged under without cutting the nets off. The submarine skipper was later relieved of his command.

In November, 1990, a British nuclear submarine snagged the net of a fishing boat near the coast of Scotland and dragged it under. All four fishermen on board drowned. London newspapers reported that in the past few years, 16 fishing vessels have been sunk by submarines, with dozens of lives lost. The British navy denies the incidents. □

Weather

Sailing, more than any other sport, involves the weather. Sailors must use the weather to their advantage, and must meet the weather on its own terms, regardless of conditions. While a hiker or skier can find shelter from a severe mountain storm, a sailor must cope until the storm abates or the voyage is over. Moreover, I have never seen a storm in the mountains that even approaches the uncertainty and danger that a storm at sea can bring. Not only do the winds change, but the playing field begins to move, sometimes dangerously so.

Weather is defined as the conditions of the atmosphere. In other words, it's about the air—whether it's moving around, wet or dry, and warm or cold.

Great storms are all forms of a cyclone. A hurricane is a cyclone in the Atlantic Ocean, with winds greater than 73 miles per hour. A typhoon is a hurricane in the Pacific. Tornadoes, found usually on land in Australia and in the central United States, are the most violent storms of all, with winds reaching up to 260 miles per hour. All storms in the northern hemisphere rotate counterclockwise. All storms in the southern hemisphere rotate clockwise (the same as water draining out of a sink or tub).

Forecasting

Despite all the hardware that has been put up in space, and all the computer-simulated models of weather patterns that have been developed, the accuracy of weather forecasting has made few, if any, advances in the past few decades. The reason we imagine that weather forecasting is an exact science is because of television, where forecasters are paid huge salaries to tell us basically inaccurate information that involved no original forecasting on their part.

Nearly all television stations receive their information daily from the National Weather Service, complete with predictions. The stations dress up the information in fancy presentations designed to suggest that their forecast is better and more accurate than someone else's—but they are all the same, and at that, not very good.

The old timers, especially the fishermen and farmers, had weather figured out better than all our modern computers and weather satellites! Old weather books, like *Eric Sloan's Weatherbook,* have taught me more about predicting sailing conditions than anything I have learned from television.

The old timers just looked around. Little things you can see for yourself tell a lot. In the morning, if there's dew on the ground or on your windshield, it won't rain today. If it rained during the night and stopped by 7 A.M., the skies will be clear by 11 A.M. Otherwise, it will rain most of the day. If the birds are flying low, particularly across the water, or if smoke from a chimney drops down low, a storm is building.

On a bigger scale, the wind tells you a lot. Because of geographical conditions, some localities may differ. But generally, if the wind is out of the west, the weather will be clear. If the wind is out of the east, the weather will turn stormy. If the wind is out of the north, the temperature will drop. If the wind is out of the south, the temperature will rise.

Farmers watch animals for signs. If livestock put on an exceptionally heavy coat of winter fur, the winter will be long and cold. Migrating birds, like geese, are foolproof harbingers of an early winter or late spring. On the other hand, I have never understood Puxatawney Phil, the Pennsylvania groundhog. Legend says that when he emerges from his den each Groundhog Day, February 2, and sees his shadow, then there will be six more weeks of winter. Six weeks later is mid-March. Isn't it always winter in mid-March? What happens if he doesn't see his shadow? The winter will last longer. Doesn't it always?

For us amateurs, two inexpensive instruments offer us the greatest help in predicting the weather—a barometer which measures the atmospheric pressure, and a thermometer which measures the air temperature. If both are rising, clear fine weather is on the way. If both are falling, hard cold weather is on the way. If the barometer is falling and the thermometer is rising, rain is on the way. If the barometer is rising and the thermometer is falling, a very clear, crisp day is on hand. With both these instruments, the rate of change is equally important, for predicting the intensity of the oncoming weather.

Clouds can be your window into the upper weather patterns. It's not necessary to remember all the various cloud formations, like cirrus, cumulus, and stratus. General observations will suffice. Look at the shape of the clouds. If they are soft and fluffy, they are usually evaporative clouds carrying moisture away—good weather is in store. If they are hard and sharp, or moving lower, close your windows. Color has little to do with the weather, except for the extremes of very dark or black. Because the sky is gray does not mean that it will rain. □

SAILING INTO
THE FUTURE

I n his book *Future Shock,* Alvin Toffler observed that it's not so much the changes that are occurring, but the speed with which they're taking place.

Sailing is no exception. Everything, from hull design to sail materials to sailing techniques, is changing—faster and faster.

A look at the records book is the quickest way to put this into perspective. In 1905, the three-masted schooner *Atlantic* set the record for sailing across the Atlantic Ocean, eastbound from the United States to England, in 12 days, 4 hours; average speed 10 knots. That record stood unbroken for 75 years, until 1980, when Frenchman Eric Tabarly sailed a trimaran across in 10 days, 5 hours; average speed 11.93 knots.

The next year, Tabarly's record was beaten. Another record was set three years after that, then another two years after that, again a year later and finally, in 1988, Frenchman Serge Medec sailed across in 7 days, 6.5 hours, average speed 16.4 knots—an increase of 60 percent over *Atlantic's* record. The *Atlantic's* record stood for 75 years, only to be bested six times in the next eight years.

The shattering of the boat speed record has been even more dramatic. For three hundred years, boats were designed basically the same way, with improvements in speed coming from minor tweaks in the rigging, exceptional crews, etc. The greatest quest for speed came in the

Early Yachting

An old saw of sailing says that the first race occurred as soon as the second sailboat was built. Actually, despite occasional unofficial races between ships and boats, sailing for sport and pleasure did not begin to grow popular until the sixteenth century.

Sailboats originally were utilitarian craft, employed in transportation, trade and war. The Greeks, Romans, and Egyptians may have used sailboats for pleasure, but the Dutch in the sixteenth and seventeenth centuries are considered the first yachtsmen. The word yacht comes from the Dutch word jacht—to hurry or hunt.

Interest in yachting spread from the continent to England when Charles II returned from exile in 1660 aboard the 52-foot sloop Mary. Although the Stuart King James I owned a small sailboat Disdain, Charles II is generally credited with introducing yachts to England. The first yacht club, the Water Club of Cork Harbor, Ireland, was formed in about 1720. Although the Water Club faded in and out of activity through the centuries, it survives today in a vigorous reincarnation as the Royal Cork Yacht Club. In 1770, a sailing club was formed at London's White Swan Tavern in Chelsea. It eventually became the Royal Thames Yacht Club.

In the United States, Colonel Lewis Morris of New York is credited with building the first U.S. pleasure boat—the sloop Fancy—in the early 1700s. Yachting did not exactly explode in the colonies. The second U.S. yacht, Captain George Crowninshield's 22-ton sloop Jefferson, was not built until 1801. The Jefferson was converted into a warship during the War of 1812, and Crowninshield replaced her with the luxurious Cleopatra's Barge, an 83-footer built for $50,000 in 1816.

In 1844, the New York Yacht Club (NYYC) was formed on the schooner Gimcrack, with John Cox Stevens as the first commodore. Within a few years, the NYYC dispatched the schooner America to England. On August 22, 1851, America defeated 16 British sailboats in a race around the Isle of Wight. That race proved to be a precursor of the America's Cup.

The steam engine, invented in 1763 by James Watt, became increasingly popular on ships in the 19th century, and Cornelius Vanderbilt, I, launched the first large U.S. steam yacht, the North Star, in 1855. From that time onward, yachtsmen would forever be divided into stink-potters and sailors.

late 1800s when the China tea clippers raced each other from China to the United States, competing for the higher prices paid for the first cargos to arrive. Although careers and fortunes were at stake, very few improvements in boat speed resulted. The most famous clipper ship of them all, the *Cutty Sark,* reached a speed of 17 knots.

Around the same time, Nathaniel Herreshoff, who would prove to be the greatest yacht designer of all time, began experimenting with catamarans—small daysailers with two pontoons with a mast in between. His most successful design, *Amaryllis II,* reached just better than 17 knots in 1876, which appeared to be a record for small sailing craft at that time. In 1933, a replica of *Amaryllis* broke the 20-knot barrier, an unheard-of speed at that time.

Another 30 years passed before the quest for speed took on a serious tone and sailors began to rethink the potential of multi-hulled sailboats. In 1961, the Little America's Cup was started as a race for catamarans between Britain and the United States, with winners reaching speeds of 22 and 23 knots. It has since grown into the premier speed event for catamarans from all over the world.

In 1972, the first speed trials to accurately measure the world's speed record in a sailboat were held in Portland, England. Boats could sail any point of sail they wished across a circle one-half kilometer (about one-third mile) in diameter. Two Brits showed up with *Crossbow,* a 60-foot outrigger canoe with a 27-foot outrigger attached to the starboard side. It could sail only on a starboard tack, but reached 26.3 knots. It had to be rowed back. In 1980, *Crossbow II,* with two asymmetrical hulls and a mast and sail on each hull, reached 36 knots.

Surfers proved to be as free-thinking as the multihulled sailors. Two Californians successfully mounted a mast on a surfboard, and their followers began tweaking the sails up to very fast speeds. In 1986, Frenchman Pascal Maka finally outsailed the multi-hulls when he took a sailboard up to 38.86 knots. Two years later, Englishman Eric Beale broke 40 knots on a sailboard in the south of France.

In the 300 years before 1933, no one had sailed faster than 20 knots. Fifty years later, that speed was doubled.

Today, new boat designs are fresh, provocative, and exciting. Designers are willing to try unorthodox methods that fly in the face of tradition, and to use exotic new materials coming out of the space and aeronautical industries.

The focus of nearly all innovation today is not the cost or comfort, but the increased speed. This is being addressed in two major thrusts—by minimizing the heeling action of a boat, thus keeping the sails as powerful as possible; and by strengthening a boat while reducing its weight.

Ever since sailors first learned to sail into the wind, they have tried to compensate for the power lost when a boat heels over. Reefing a sail down helps solve the heeling problem, but reducing sail area decreases power. Herreshoff's solution of a boat with two skinny hulls spaced widely apart was such a radical design—and so resoundingly faster—that the sailing community banned it, as not an acceptable design.

Traditional sailors approached the heeling problem by adding deeper and heavier keels, until boats became unrealistically heavy and required clouds of sail. Some of the America's Cup defenders built around the turn of the century carried more than 10,000 square feet of sail, and required crews of more than 100 men.

Only recently have traditional sailors begun to accept the obvious advantages of multihulls, with their inherent stabilty and incredible speeds. By keeping the sails upright in the wind, and reducing the weight of the hulls, catamarans and trimarans can double and sometimes triple the speed of conventional monohull. Monohull sailors argue that catamarans cannot be righted once flipped over, are too wide for marinas, and are aesthetically ugly. On the other hand, monohulls readily sink when swamped, whereas cats will float upside down.

Hobie Alter, a surfboard manufacturer in Southern California, popularized catamarans in the 1960s when he introduced his Hobie Cats, very fast 14-foot and 16-foot catamarans that were easy to sail, beach, and trailer.

The French have always been believers in multihulls and were the first to begin sailing them across oceans. Today, French multihulls are in the vanguard of speed and distance records. A large French cat now holds the record for a trans-Atlantic crossing of 7 days, averaging nearly 17 knots.

The first formal acceptance by Americans of large multihulls came in 1988 when Dennis Conner sailed a 60-foot catamaran against New Zealand's 130-foot monohull to successfully defend the America's Cup in San Diego.

Despite all the advances in design and materials, propulsion by sail is inefficient; most sailmakers and naval architects agree that only about 20 percent of the power generated by sails is directed toward making the boat go forward. The big factors holding down boat speed are hull resistance against the water and the boat's tendency to heel.

Landsailers—three-wheeled carts with a mast and sail—
heel very little and have almost no surface friction to
combat; consequently, they have reached speeds of nearly
90 miles per hour. Iceboats, with greater stability because
of wider runners with even less surface friction, have
sailed four to five times the speed of the actual wind. The
speed record for a sail-powered vessel is 143 miles per
hour, set in 1938 in Wisconsin. These two types of hard-
surface skimmers show that an airfoil can develop tremendous power. The problem with a boat lies in the disadvantage of trying to go fast in water.

One of the earliest, and most successful, attempts at stability and speed was in the 1970s when Rod Johnstone
began designing his "J" boats—J-22s, J-24s, J-35s and now
J-44s. These awkward looking racers had an extremely
wide beam amidships. The extra width gave tremendous
stability and, with the correct contours, actually increased
the waterline length of the boat when it heeled over. J-
Boats are very fast and stable, and today the J-24 and J-35
racing classes are the most active in the country.

Garry Hoyt, a progressive-thinking designer who drew
the plans for the popular Freedom yachts, has now introduced a radical compromise between a monohull and a
multi-hull. His new Manta Clipper is a 34-foot monohull
sloop with "wingfins"—wings extending out from the
back half of the hull and gradually bending downward
into pontoons. It has a 14-foot beam, a flat bottom aft,
and, without ballast in the keel, weighs only 7,500
pounds. Hoyt added other innovations, such as an A-
frame mast which places the stress of a mast on the outer
hull instead of on the keel, and roller-furling jib and main

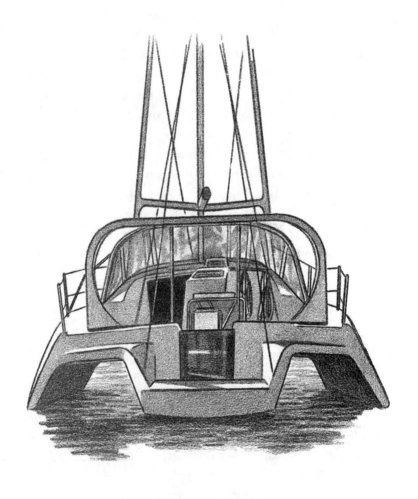

sails. To appeal to the weekend cruising crowd, Hoyt installed a very large, 120-horsepower engine (about three times normal power) which enables the boat to plane at 14 knots under power. Thus, a family could conceivably motor 60 or 70 miles home on a Sunday afternoon.

The biggest drawback of the Manta Clipper is that the wide, flat bottom makes the boat ride poorly in large seas. But Hoyt says you don't want to be out in such conditions—the reason he put in such a large engine!

A large, cooperative solution to the problems of both stability and weight reduction has resulted in an experimental 65-foot sloop, *Amoco Procyon,* an innovative design conceived by Olaf and Peter Harken, a yacht hardware manufacturer; naval architect Britton Chance; a number of sailing manufacturers; with an overall sponsorship by Amoco Chemical.

Amoco Procyon has a number of experimental projects on board. The most revolutionary is a canting bulb keel, which can be pivoted up the windward side as much as 25 degrees. If the boat is heeling 20 degrees, the keel extends 45 degrees below the plane of the water. By moving the center of gravity out to the windward side, the boat rights itself into the wind, increasing the power of the sails.

However, with the keel at a 45 degree angle, it loses its ability to resist the boat's leeway, or slippage to the side caused by the wind. So designer Chance installed two, four-foot winglets extending perpendicularly out from the bottom of the keel. As the keel approaches a horizontal position, the eight-foot wing approaches a vertical position and resists the leeway.

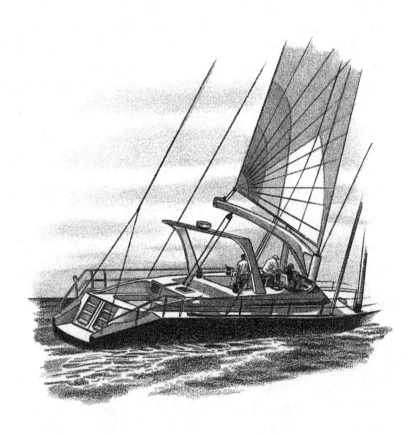

Amoco Procyon also has water ballast tanks on both sides of the hull, which can be filled when to windward and emptied when to leeward. Redistributing the two tons of water has a significant effect on stabilizing the boat.

In an attempt to redistribute the forces of the mast, Chance also designed an A-frame mast made of lightweight, superstrong carbon fiber. Conventional masts exert tremendous downward pressure where they rest on the keel, while the side shrouds tend to lift up the edges of the hull where they're attached to chainplates. The A-frame design eliminates the shrouds and places the downward force of the mast out on the edges of the hull, a compression load which makes the hull stronger and safer. The mainsail is attached to a cable, which runs vertically between the masthead and the keel. This cable is put under tremendous tension, to hold the luff of the sail tight, and futher increases the compression load of the hull by pulling the mast down and the keel up.

The mast is made out of carbon fiber, and weighs approximately half as much as an equivalent aluminum mast. Less weight aloft further aides the stability of the boat. Carbon fiber is also extremely strong, particularly under compression.

Both the genoa and the mainsail are roller-furling, controlled by the skipper from the cockpit. Because roller-furling is such an easy and quick method for reducing sail area in a blow, Chance designed the boat to carry up to about 2,000 square feet of sail—roughly 40 percent more than normal. The extra sail area is an advantage in light winds. Harken and Chance estimate that overall, *Amoco Procyon* is 10 to 15 percent faster than a

Sailing with Kids

Sailing is an adventure-filled sport, and children love adventure. The sea presents a plethora of natural wonders, with fish, birds, shells and other delights. The dinghy is a child-size yacht and provides the child with an excellent method for exploring the shoreline. A 100-foot line attached to the bow as a tether will also provide parents with peace of mind.

Sailboats themselves are intrinsically interesting for kids and are filled with amusing objects. Whereas a piece of rope could entrance a young child, older children can help with the sails. Children may adapt easily to shipboard life. That claustrophobic quarterberth can be a cozy hideaway for a child, and the generally cramped spaces of a sailboat seem relatively spacious to kids.

The caveat to sailing with children is safety. Many sailors string netting along their lifelines, which leaves a boat looking like a giant playpen. Don't forget, though, that toddlers are able to climb the netting. Some parents take car seats on their boats, and harnesses are a good idea for children on deck. Life preservers are a must on or near the water. Only use life preservers with collars that keep a child's head afloat, face up. No safety system can replace parental supervision. Any child on a boat should know how to swim.

conventional sloop of the same size.

Another example of throwing out conventional wisdom is the experimental boat *Just Do It,* a 70-footer designed by two Californians, Alberto Calderon and Charles Robinson. They reasoned that it's wrong to design a keel both to provide righting moment and to resist leeway. They say the keel provides the greatest righting moment when it's nearly horizontal, and the greatest leeway resistance when it's vertical.

So they added two long, slender, foil-shaped appendages to the bottom of *Just Do It,* one near the forward tip of the waterline and one near the aft end of the waterline. They also installed a keel amidship, with the majority of its weight in a bulb at the bottom. The keel can be canted up to 60 degrees from its vertical position, or 30 degrees below the plane of the water, with the boat upright. During pronounced heeling (more than 30 degrees), they can actually pull the bulb up above the surface of the water.

The keel now works only to counteract the heeling force, while the two foils, whose shapes can be changed underway, work both to counteract leeway and to steer the boat.

Calderon and Robinson are optimistic that this type of experimentation will enable designers to beat the "hull speed" limitation with radical hull designs that will not create trough waves. They say one design they are looking into is a long, slender canoe body. They'll design it with a very wide deck, which, besides adding crew comfort, would serve as emergency pontoons.

Some new ideas must start out small. Experimental

sailors like Chris Lloyd are now transferring sailboard design features back to small centerboard boats. Lloyd's design has two moveable yet rigid stays, which form a tripod with the mast, eliminating all wire rigging. This design enables a single person to trim the mast fore and aft, depending on boat speed and wind speed, while hiking out. Lloyd has also moved the rudder forward to just aft of the bow, which he considers a far more efficient location for steering.

Other, less radical, cruising designs have also eliminated the wire rigging: forestays, backstays and sidestays. Garry Hoyt's Freedom yachts have unstayed masts, no jibs and the mainsails have wishbone booms. Nonsuch yachts have a similar design. Both have proved to be very popular with cruisers and charterers because the sails are so easy to tend. These boats are, in their simplicity, in marked contrast to the clutter and endless yards of rigging on the old schooners of 50 years ago.

The challenge now is to take Lloyd's trimmable mast and put it on a cruising boat of 30 to 40 feet. Perhaps the A-frame will be the answer. Add a canting keel and moveable ballast and sailboat designs have grown into a new generation.

Sailing, for all the current interest in space-age, man-made materials, is a sport almost entirely compatible with the environment.

Some elements of sailing do not treat the land, air and water well: outboard engines and small diesel auxiliaries, the shoreline taken up by marinas, and the pollution caused by the manufacture and eventual disposal of sailboat materials. But these elements are changing.

More and more fiberglass and plastics are being shredded for recycling back into other compounds, roadbase materials, and insulation. With recycling to handle the problem of discarded fiberglass, the boating industry is rapidly moving into widespread use of composites for nearly every part of a boat, from hulls to masts, rudders and keels, even deck hardware and winch handles. Top-of-the-line racing boats use only a fractional amount of the metal they used just a few years ago.

Tougher environmental standards are forcing boat yards to use new building techniques, such as vacuum bagging, which reduces styrene emissions, a major pollutant in polyester resins. And more and more of the poisonous chemicals found in boat yards, such as resins, solvents, adhesives and paints, are now water-based.

But the fundamental environmental advantage of sailboats is that they're as natural today as they were thousands of years ago. For the most part, a sailboat navigates through its world of wind and water leaving not a single trace of its passage. Nothing is consumed. Nothing is altered. The water and the winds are left in exactly the same condition for the next user. Sailing is forever.

COMPETITION
Olympic Yachting

Sailing is one of the most athletically democratic sports in the Olympics.

Men and women compete against each other, sailors do not have to be genetic masterpieces, and competitors, although most are in their twenties and thirties, have ranged in age from teenagers to sixty-year-olds. Denmark's Paul Elvström is a model of longevity; he has competed in eight Olympics and became the first sailor to win four gold medals. The boats are also relatively affordable—the largest Olympic-class boat is the 26'9" Soling—so championship campaigns never approach the multi-million dollar extravaganzas of America's Cup races.

Sailing was added to the Olympics in 1900 and has been included in all but the 1904 St. Louis Games when there was no suitable racing site. The races are held on closed, triangular courses, typically on large inland lakes or the ocean. The boats race in fleets—all the boats in each race are of the same class and there is no need for handicapping. The winner is the first boat across the line.

There are eight one-design sailing classes in the Olympics. One-design boats conform to uniform standards for construction, materials, size, and weight.

In order of ascending size, the classes begin with the 11-foot **Europe** dinghy. The newest boat in the Olympics, it was added for the 1992 Games and is for women only. The Europe weighs less than 100 pounds and carries a skipper and one sail. The Europe is well-suited for women because it works best with a skipper weighing between 100 and 170 pounds.

The 12' **Lechner Division II** sailboard is also relatively new to Olympic competition.

Europe

Sailboards, the fastest monohull sailing craft, first appeared in the 1984 Olympics, and the Lechner replaced the orig-

Lechner Division II

inal Windglider in the 1988 Games. A speedy board, the Lechner is divided into men's and women's divisions. Ideally, sailboarders are tall and agile.

The 14'9" **Finn**, quite appropriately, was designed by Finnish sailer Rickard Sarby and became an Olympic class for the 1952 Games in Helsinki. It has been part of the Games ever since, making it the longest continually used sailboat in Olympic competition. A singlehander with one sail, the Finn requires great strength. Finn sailors are typically large, and they often wear weighted

Finn

vests carrying as much as 40 pounds.

The **470** gets its name from its length—470 centimeters (15'5"). The 470 joined the Olympics in 1976, and a separate class for women was added in 1988. Allison Jolly and Lynne Jewell-Shore sailed a 470 to the only U.S. sailing gold medal in 1988. A two-person, centerboard boat that carries a main, jib and spinnaker, the 470 is a planing dinghy. With more than 30,000 sailers worldwide, the 470 is one of the most popular Olympic boats.

470

A 19'10" centerboard boat, the **Flying Dutchman** has a reputation for being a fast boat. It carries a crew of two and a main, spinnaker and jib. It entered the Olympics in 1960 and is an open class for men and women.

Flying Dutchman

While multihull designs have grown increasingly faster and more high-tech every year, the relatively staid **Tornado** has, with a few modifications, been the Olympic multihull since its addition in 1976. Staid is no

Tornado

synonym for slow—the Tornado is among the fastest of the sailboats in the Olympics and has a top speed of about 30 knots. The open-class Tornado, a 20' catamaran, carries two sails and a two-person crew.

Star

The 22'8" **Star** has, with the exception of 1976, been an Olympic class since 1932, which makes it the most frequently raced of the Olympic classes. It is also the oldest one-design sailboat, with roots that stretch back to 1910. A two-person crew mans the Star, a keelboat with a flat bottom and two sails. Past and present America's Cup skippers Dennis Conner, Buddy Melges and the late Tom Blackaller sailed Stars. It is an open class.

The **Soling** is the queen of the Olympic fleet. It carries a crew of three, and, at 2,281 pounds and nearly 27 feet, is considerably larger than the other boats. A keelboat with a relatively large 355-square foot spinnaker, the Soling joined the Olympics in 1972. Numerous famous sailors including Elvström, John Kolius and Robbie Haines have sailed the Soling, and it is a common choice for yacht clubs and day-sailers. It is an open class. □

Soling

America's Cup

The America's Cup is boating's most prestigious award and one of the sporting world's oldest prizes.

In 1851 when the schooner *America* sailed to England and beat sixteen British yachts in a series of sailing races, the prize was a rather garish looking Hundred Guinea Cup. This later became known as the *America's* Cup. In 1870, the English asked for and were granted a chance to regain the Cup. They sent over their fastest yacht, *Cambria,* which raced against twenty-three American yachts. *Cambria* finished tenth; *America,* the original challenger, finished fourth; and the schooner *Magic* won.

The Deed of Gift for the America's Cup, written in 1857 and revised in 1881 and 1887, provided the ground rules for the competition. The New York Yacht Club issued a challenge: nations worldwide could compete against the United States in a series of yacht races. The NYYC hosted the races in Newport, Rhode Island. Any successful challenger could hold the next series of races in its home port.

Any country may enter a boat to challenge for the Cup. Those entries sail a series of round-robin races, with the winner emerging as the challenger. Anyone from the defending country may enter a boat into another round-robin series of eliminations to determine the defending boat. After both boats are chosen, they sail against each other in a best-of-seven series.

The uniqueness of America's Cup races is the format of match racing: there are only two boats matched against each other. This develops into a very different sort of sailboat race, unlike fleet racing where everyone sails as fast as possible for the finish line.

In match racing, tactics are more important than pure boat speed. Occasionally the slower boat will win because the crew handled the sails better or because the tactician and skipper were craftier. The starts often resemble bizarre mating dances as the two boats attempt to cover each other's air, giving the upwind boat the advantage of clear air. Tacking duels to windward may drag both boats well off the layline to the next mark. Once the lead boat develops a comfortable lead, it may mimic the following boat, including running off course to prevent the following boat from discovering a fresh breeze or stronger current that could carry it to the next mark ahead of the leader.

The classes of boats have changed a number of times over the years, with the boats getting larger and larger around the turn of the century as owners opened their bank accounts wide. In the 1930s, the J-boats were brought in as spectacular racing vessels—135 feet on deck with a single mast taller than a 12-story building. In the late 1950s and early 1960s, the race committee settled on a more conventional 12-meter design in order to keep the costs from spiraling up. These boats were designed to a complicated formula involving eight different measurements totaling 12 meters. The boats were about 67 feet in length.

The United States successfully defended the Cup 23 times over 132 years. It finally changed hands in 1983 when

Australian Alan Bond and his crew finally captured "ye auld mug." Bond, who spent a large fortune over nine years chasing the Cup, promptly filled it with champagne and took it down under.

American Dennis Conner won the Cup back in Australia in 1987 and brought it to his San Diego Yacht Club. In the 1988 series in San Diego, challenger New Zealand, claiming a loophole in the racing rules, brought out a 130 foot high-tech sloop. Connor responded with a 60-foot catamaran, which easily outsailed New Zealand and kept the Cup in the United States.

To eliminate extremes of design for the 1992 America's Cup, the race committee established the America's Cup class—sloops measuring 75 feet overall, a waterline length of 57 feet, displacement of 42,000 pounds and a sail area of 3,200 square feet. It is still a very expensive avocation: William Koch, of the America 3 campaign, spent in excess of $45 million for the chance to defend the Cup.

America's Cup Results

Year	Defender (Skipper)	Challenger (Country)	Result
1870	*Magic* (J. Tannock)	*Cambria* (UK)	1-0
1871	*Columbia* (Nelson Comstock)	*Livonia* (UK)	4-1
	Sappho (Sam Greenwood)		
1876	*Madeleine* (Josephus Williams)	*Countess of Dufferin* (Can)	2-0
1881	*Mischief* (Nathaniel Clock)	*Atalanta* (Can)	2-0
1885	*Puritan* (Aubrey Crocker)	*Genesta* (UK)	2-0
1886	*Mayflower* (Martin Stone)	*Galatea* (UK)	2-0
1887	*Volunteer* (Henry Haff)	*Thistle* (UK)	2-0
1893	*Vigilant* (William Hansen)	*Valkyrie II* (UK)	3-0
1895	*Defender* (Henry Haff)	*Valkyrie III* (UK)	3-0
1899	*Columbia* (Charles Barr)	*Shamrock I* (UK)	3-0
1901	*Columbia* (Charles Barr)	*Shamrock II* (UK)	3-0
1903	*Reliance* (Charles Barr)	*Shamrock III* (UK)	3-0
1920	*Resolute* (Charles Francis Adams)	*Shamrock IV* (UK)	3-2
1930	*Enterprise* (Harold Vanderbilt)	*Shamrock V* (UK)	4-0
1934	*Rainbow* (Harold Vanderbilt)	*Endeavour* (UK)	4-2
1937	*Ranger* (Harold Vanderbilt)	*Endeavour II* (UK)	4-0
1958	*Columbia* (Briggs Cunningham)	*Sceptre* (UK)	4-0
1962	*Weatherly* (Bus Mosbacher)	*Gretel* (Australia)	4-1
1964	*Constellation* (Robert Bavier & Eric Ridder)	*Sovereign* (UK)	4-0
1967	*Intrepid* (Bus Mosbacher)	*Dame Pattie* (Aus)	4-0
1970	*Intrepid* (Bill Ficker)	*Gretel II* (Aus)	4-1
1974	*Courageous* (Ted Hood)	*Southern Cross* (Aus)	4-0
1977	*Courageous* (Ted Turner)	*Australia* (Aus)	4-0
1980	*Freedom* (Dennis Conner)	*Australia* (Aus)	4-1
1983	*Liberty* (Dennis Conner)	*Australia II* (Aus)	3-4
1987	*Kookaburra II* (Iain Murray)	*Stars and Stripes* (US)	0-4
1988	*Stars and Stripes* (Dennis Conner)	*New Zealand* (NZ)	2-0

Sailing Records

This is the list of record passages on a number of established race courses and some traditional routes that attract individual speed attempts. It is for information only and has been compiled over a number of years from different sources. Suggested amendments and additions should be sent to the Secretary, IYRU/World Sailing Speed Record Council.

Race/Route	Dist. (Nautical Miles)	ElapsedTime	Date
★Transatlantic W to E Ambrose Light to Lizard Point	2,925	6d13h3m32s	6/90
★Transatlantic W to E Ambrose Light to Lizard Point (single-hull)	2,925	8d3h29m	7/88
★Round Isle of Wight ("*America's*" Course) Easterly	49.65	3h42m32s	8/86
Transpacific (Los Angeles–Honolulu)	2,225	6d22h41m2s	8/89

Key to Types

IOR	IOR-class yacht
ULDB	Ultralight displacement yacht
T	Trimaran
C	Catamaran
M	Multihull (configuration not known)
S	Single-hulled yacht, neither IOR nor ULDB
(1)	Voyage was single-handed; otherwise boat had two or more people

Yacht	Type	LOA (ft./m)	Owner/ Skipper	Speed (Ave. Knots)
Jet Services V	C	75/22.80	Serge Medec (France)	18.62
Phocea	S	244/74.37	Bernard Tapie (France)	14.96
Roger Et Gallet	C	75/22.86	Eric Loiseau (France)	13.48
Aikane X-5	C	62/18.90	Rudy Choy (U.S.A)	13.34

Race/Route	Dist. (Nautical Miles)	ElapsedTime	Date
Chicago–Mackinac	333	1d1h50m44s	7/87
Marblehead–Halifax	360	1d9h29m57s	7/89
Round World Whitbread Course 1989-90 5 Stops	32,932	128d9h40m30s	9/89–5/90
*Round Britain and Ireland (All Islands)	1,950	7d19h30m	7/89
Newport–Bermuda	635	2d14h29m	1982
Fastnet Race	605	2d12h41m15s	8/85
Round World 4 Stops Newport–Newport (BOC Race)	27,000	120d22h36m35s	9/90–4/91
Los Angeles–Tahiti	3,600	17d7h58m	6/64

Yacht	Type	LOA (ft./m)	Owner/ Skipper	Speed (Ave. Knots)
Pied Piper	IOR	67/20.42	Dick Jennings (U.S.A)	12.88
Starlight Express II	IOR	70/21.3	Bruce Eissner (U.S.A.)	10.74
Steinlager II	IOR	84/25.60	Peter Blake (New Zealand)	10.69
Saab Turbo	C	75/22.86	Francois Bouchier (France)	10.40
Nirvana	IOR	80/24.38	(U.S.A)	10.16
Nirvana	IOR	80/24.38	Marvin Green (U.S.A)	9.97
Groupe Sceta	S(1)	60/18.3	Christophe Auguin (France)	9.30
Ticonderoga	CCA	72/21.94	Bob Johnson (U.S.A.)	8.65

Race/Route	Dist. (Nautical Miles)	ElapsedTime	Date
Rio-Newport	5,000	26d0h50m20s	1987
*New York to San Francisco Via Cape Horn	13,945	76d23h20m	3/89– 5/89

IYRU/WSSRC World Records as of October, 1991
*IYRU/WSSRC recognized world record passages

500-Meter Course World Records

Class	Name	Country
Women's	Babethe Coquelle	France
Outright	Thierry Bielak	France

Sailing speed records are ratified and compiled by the IYRU/World Sailing Speed Record Council.

Yacht	Type	LOA (ft./m)	Owner/ Skipper	Speed (Ave. Knots)
Tuna Marine	S(1)	60/18.3	John Martin (U.S.A.)	8.00
Great American	T	60/18.29	George Kolesnikov (U.S.A.)	7.55

Speed	Date	Location
39.70 knots	7/91	Tarifa, Spain
44.66 knots	4/91	St. Maries, France

GLOSSARY

Aft—toward the back of the boat.

Aground—stuck on the bottom.

Aid to navigation—charted mark to assist navigators, such as buoys, lights, lighthouses and channel markers.

Alee—away from the direction of the wind.

Aloft—up in the rigging or up the mast.

Amidships—toward the center of the boat.

Anemometer—instrument that measures wind speed.

Astern—behind the back of the boat.

Aweigh—when the anchor is clear of the bottom.

Backstays—support cables that run from the top of the mast to the stern.

Ballast—weight placed in the bottom of the boat to provide stability.

Bark—three-masted boat, fore and mainmasts square rigged, mizzenmast fore-and-aft rigged.

Barkentine—three-masted sailboat, with a square-rigged foremast and fore-and-aft rigged main and mizzenmasts.

Beacon—navigation light, usually placed on land or other obstructions as a warning; also a directional radio beam used for navigation.

Beam—width of a boat at its widest point.

Bearing—angle of direction toward an object, relative to boat's direction.

Beaufort scale—scale of wind velocities that ranges from 0 (flat calm) to 12 (hurricane).

Bell buoy—a buoy with a bell that rings when the waves move the buoy.

Bend—fasten with a knot.

Bermuda rig—fore-and-aft rig with triangular sails, also known as Marconi rig.

Bilge—the lowest interior area in a boat's hull.

Binnacle—a compass mounting.

Block—a pulley, or sheave, used to change the direction of a line or rope.

Boom—the spar that extends the foot of the sail and to which the foot is attached.

Bow—the front of a boat.

Bow line—mooring line at front of boat.

Bowline—knot used to form a loop that will not slip.

Bowsprit—permanent spar attached to the bow to which jibstays and forestays are fastened.

Bridge—control station of a boat, often enclosed.

Brigantine—two-masted boat with square-rigged foremast and fore-and-aft rigged mainmast.

Brightwork—varnished wood on boat.

Bring about—to change direction.

Broach—to swing broadside into the wind, usually as a result of losing control in heavy seas, and sometimes resulting in an involuntary jibe.

Broad reach—to sail with wind between quarter and beam.

Bulkhead—a below-decks fortification or partition in the hull of a boat.

Buoy—a floating marker anchored in place to indicate a channel or mooring.

Burgee—yacht club flag, usually triangular.

Catamaran—twin-hulled boat.

Catboat—a wide, shallow-draft sloop with the mast just aft of the bow, eliminating the jib.

Centerboard—a wide, flat board that can be raised and lowered to counteract leeway.

Cleat—a fitting of wood, metal or both, with horns to which lines are fastened.

Close hauled—sailing at as high an angle into the wind as possible, also known as "beating."

Come about—to bring the boat through the wind from one tack to the other.

Daggerboard—removable centerboard.

Dead reckoning—informal tracking of vessel's position, based on speed and direction.

Deviation—compass error caused by magnetic fields.

Displacement—weight of a boat, measured in terms of the water it displaces.

Draft—depth of a boat from waterline to lowest point of keel or motor.

Ease off—to fall slightly off the wind; or to slack a line or boat speed.

Fathom—nautical depth measuring six feet, known as a "half twain" in Mississippi River parlance, 100 fathoms make a cable.

Following sea—waves coming from the rear of the boat.

Forestay—a support cable running from the foredeck to the mast, supports the jib.

Furl—to roll up and secure a sail to a stay or boom.

Gaff—the spar that supports the top edge of a four-sided mainsail; also spar that can hold flags.

Galley—boat's kitchen.

Genoa—a large jib that overlaps the mainsail.

Gimbal—levelling device used to keep stove and compass upright when boat heels.

Ground tackle—equipment associated with the anchor.

Gunkholing—coastal cruising, consisting of a series of short trips between harbors or anchorages.

Hatch—an opening from the deck into the interior of a boat.

Head—a boat's toilet, also the top corner of a sail.

Heading—direction the bow is pointing.

Headsails—sails set in front of the foremast.

Heave to—to turn into the wind and reduce or eliminate sail in a storm.

Heel—the tilt or laying over of a boat, caused by wind.

Helm—steering station (tiller or wheel) of a boat.

Hike—to lean out over the windward rail to counteract heel on a small boat.

Hull speed—a sailboat's theoretical top speed in knots, calculated by multiplying the square root of waterline length by 1.4.

In irons—facing into the wind, unable to make headway.

Jib—triangular headsail set on forestay or headstay.

Jibe—to change directions with the wind behind the boat.

Kedge—an auxiliary anchor; or maneuver in which anchor is carried away from boat that has run aground and then used to pull the boat free by "kedging off".

Keel—central backbone of a boat, a longitudinal timber attached to the hull; or external ballast at the bottom of a boat.

Ketch—a two-masted boat in which the aft mast, the mizzenmast, is shorter than the forward mast and is located ahead of the rudder post.

Knot—a nautical mile per hour (a nautical mile is 6,080 feet); also a bend, hitch or splice.

Lee shore—downwind shore.

Leeward—away from the direction of the wind, sometimes pronounced lu-ard.

Leeway—sidewise slippage of boat through water away from wind.

Lifeline—lines strung around deck from stanchions, for safety of the crew.

Line—the generic term for all ropes used on a boat.

List—a boat's lean caused by an on-board weight imbalance rather than wind or waves.

LOA—length of a boat at its longest point.

Locker—the closets and other storage areas aboard a boat.

Log—speed measuring device attached to the stern of boat.

Logbook—a boat's diary, records a boat's activities.

Loran—long range aid to navigation, a navigational system receiving signals sent from land-based transmitting stations.

Luff—the forward edge of a sail, "luffing" occurs when a boat comes into the wind and the sails flutter.

LWL—length of a boat along the water line.

Mainsail—the sail attached to the main, or largest, mast on a boat.

Main sheet—the line used to control the mainsail, attached to the main boom.

Make fast—to attach a line or rope securely.

Marconi rig—sail configuration that uses triangular sails fore and aft, also called Bermuda rig.

Marlinspike—a pointed instrument, often part of a sailor's knife, used for splicing rope.

Mast—vertical spar used to support sails and booms.

Mayday—radio distress call, derived from the French *m'aidez,* "help me."

Midships—in the center of the boat.

Mizzen—the after mast on a ketch or yawl.

Mizzen sail—the sail on the after mast of a ketch or yawl.

Motor sailer—a combination motor boat and sailboat,

that is roomier with a larger engine than a typical sailboat.

Offshore wind—wind blowing from land out to sea, usually in mornings.

One-design boats—racing sailboats built to the same specifications and with the same materials.

Outboard—off the rail, projecting over the water; or an auxiliary engine attached to the stern.

Permanent backstay—support cable running from stern to top of mast.

Pitch—the bobbing motion of a boat from bow to stern caused by waves.

Pitchpole—to somersault, usually in high seas.

Planing—riding on top of the water, which allows a boat to exceed hull speed.

Planing hull—hull designed to ride on top of the water at high speeds.

Plot—to find one's course and position on a chart.

Pooped—to have a wave break over the stern.

Port—the left side of the boat, looking toward the bow, or a circular window.

Privileged vessel—boat with the right of the way.

Quarter—the section of a boat from amidships to the stern.

Reckoning—calculation of a boat's position.

Reef—to reduce the working area of a sail by partially furling it, usually done in heavy weather.

Reef knot—square knot.

Regatta—a series of boat races with cumulative scores kept.

Ride—lie smoothly at anchor.

Rigging—the apparatus used to support and operate the mast and sails; standing rigging is stationary, includes spars, stays and turnbuckles, and support the mast; running rigging moves, includes sheets and halyards, and is used to control the sails.

Rode—anchor line and/or chain.

Rudder—a broad, thin appendage attached underwater.

Schooner—a boat with two or more masts, with the forewardmost, the foremast, shorter than the aftermost, the mainmast.

Scope—the ratio of anchor rode to water depth, typically five to seven.

Scow—flat-bottom boat with a blunt prow.

Scupper—a hole in the rail or gunwale that allows water drainage.

Sextant—celestial-navigation instrument that triangulates boat's position against heavenly bodies.

Sheet—line used to control a sail.

Shoal—shallow water, or obstruction in shallow water, such as coral.

Sloop—boat with a single mast and a single headsail.

Sound—to measure the depth of water.

Soundings—depth measurements.

Spar—a mast, boom, gaff, spreader or spinnaker pole.

Spinnaker—a large, light, triangular sail for downwind sailing.

Splice—to connect two ropes or cables by weaving

threads of each together.

Spreaders—horizontal spars, attached to mast, that spread shrouds and give them added angulation.

Springlines—dock lines set to prevent forward and backward motion.

Square-rigged—boat with four-sided sails.

Standing rigging—the permanent wires and fittings used to support the mast.

Starboard—the right side of the boat, looking toward the bow.

Stay—the cables that support a mast fore and aft, head-stays, forestays and backstays.

Staysail—a small headsail set between the jib and the mast.

Stern—the back end of a boat.

Storm sails—small, heavy sails for use in high wind.

Tack—to sail to windward by zig-zagging, staying as close to the wind as possible, or the forward, bottom corner of a sail.

Telltale—a piece of yarn, ribbon or something light attached to a sail or shroud and used to indicate wind direction.

Tender—a boat that heels too easily; also a small boat used to ferry people to a boat at a mooring.

Tide—periodic rise and fall of ocean waters, caused by pull of sun and moon's gravity on earth.

Tiller—a long bar attached to rudder and used for steering.

Topside—the deck; or that part of the hull above the waterline.

Transom—the stern facing of the hull.

Trapeze—a harness attached to the mast, used by small-boat sailers to suspend their weight outboard to windward.

Trimaran—boat with three hulls.

Under the lee—protected from the wind.

Waterline—painted line on the hull that indicates where the boat rides in the water.

Weather side—side of boat on which wind is blowing.

Windlass—winch used to maneuver anchor.

Working sails—mainsail and jib, the sails used in normal conditions.

Yacht—a pleasure boat.

Yawl—two-masted boat with mizzenmast mounted behind rudder post and shorter than the main mast. □

BOOKS AND VIDEOS
FOR GOOD READING

Sailing Alone Around the World, by Joshua Slocum, Dover Publications or Sheridan Publishing Co. The classic first-person account by the first man to sail alone around the world, in a 38-foot boat. Joshua Slocum is a folk hero in the sailing world.

Men At Sea, by Brandt Aymar, Random House. A wonderful collection of the best sea stories of all time, from Homer's *The Odyssey* through DeFoe, Conrad, London and Hemingway, from heroic captains such as John Paul Jones through the Battle of Midway.

The Big Book of Sailing, by Grubb and Richter, Barron's Education Service Inc. A large coffee-table book with superb writing about sailing, the sea, and the people who venture out. Excellent photographs.

Unfinished Voyages A Chronology of Shipwrecks, by John Perry Fish, Lower Cape Publishing Co. Fascinating account of shipwrecks along the northeast coast of America, from 1606 through the Andrea Doria in 1956. Includes a chart with dates and approximate locations of more than 500 shipwrecks.

American Sailors Treasury, by Frank Shay, Smithmark Publishing Co. A book of sea songs, chanteys, legends and lore. It includes the music and words to 76 sea songs. A wonderful companion for lots of fun once the lamp starts swinging.

ADVENTURE STORIES

Fastnet Force 10, by John Rousmaniere, W.W. Norton & Co. In history's most disastrous yacht race, the 1979 Fastnet Race, a sudden storm claimed the lives of 15 sailors lost in the Irish Sea. Countless ocean-racing yachts were abandoned or sunk. A superbly written account of the worst that can happen at sea.

Shackleton's Boat Journey, by F.A. Worsley, Collectors' Books Ltd, England; W.W. Norton & Co. The story of the 1914 expedition to cross Antarctica that ended in disaster. The author was captain of the *Endurance,* which became stuck in an ice floe and was crushed. Shackleton finally made it to safety after a 1,000-mile journey over land and in an open boat.

Venturesome Voyages, by J.C. Voss, Sheridan House. Voss circumnavigated the world at the turn of the century in a decked-in canoe. A marvelous storyteller, Voss gives enthusiastic and humorous accounts of the people and places he saw.

An Island to Oneself, by Tom Neale, Ox Bow Press. Tom Neale quit the civilized life in his fifties and moved alone to a tiny desert island in the South Pacific. This is his account of the six years he spent as a modern-day Robinson Crusoe.

HOW-TO GUIDES AND REFERENCE BOOKS

The Craft of Sail, by Jan Adkins, Walker and Co. A primer for learning to sail on small craft, with a good feel for the environment. Adkins covers much more than merely what to do, explaining why and how sailboats and equipment work. Some theory and lots of beautiful drawings. Good for kids learning to sail.

Chapman's Piloting, Seamanship, and Small Boat Handling, Sixtieth Edition; by Charles F. Chapman, William Morrow & Co. The bible of boating. It's a must and can be found on board every single ocean-going vessel. Detailed answers to every question you will have about handling your boat, from navigation to weather to safety to etiquette. What other book has a sixtieth edition?

HUMOR

The Boat Who Wouldn't Float, by Farley Mowat, Bantam Paperbacks. An outrageous story, by Canada's premier outdoor writer (*Never Cry Wolf*), of him and his pal buying a wreck of a boat in the Maritime Provinces and trying to get it down the St. Lawrence Seaway to Toronto. Perfect for the beginning sailor.

FOR KIDS

The Wind in the Willows, by Kenneth Grahame, MacMillan & Co. The classic read for kids interested in messin' about in boats. Great for adults too.

The Wreck of the Zephyr, by Chris Van Allsburg, Houghton-Mifflin Co. This is a winner of the Caldecott Medal as the best children's book of the year. A wonderful story, with beautiful illustrations, of a large schooner off on a mythical journey.

MYSTERIES AND SUSPENSE

Riddle of the Sands, by Erskine Childers, Penguin Books. For seventy years this has been the classic sailing mystery, set in the North Sea, just prior to Germany entering WWI. It combines the lore of the sea, spies and a continually twisting plot. Also available in video.

Shipkiller, by Justin Scott, Amereon. The worst fear of offshore sailing—a supertanker coldly crushes a ketch. To revenge the death of his wife and the loss of his boat, the survivor tracks the giant ship across raging seas to a confrontation in the snake-infested Persian Gulf.

WOMEN'S ADVENTURES

Maiden, by Tracy Edwards, Barnacle Press. Having crewed unglamorously for years on charter boats and racing yachts, Tracy Edwards, a former dancer, assembled an all-female crew to refurbish an ocean racer and compete in the 1990 Whitbread Around the World Race.

Maiden Voyage, by Tania Aebi, Ballantine Books. In a desperate attempt to motivate his runaway daughter, Tania's father offers to buy her a 26-foot sailboat if she will sail it alone around the world. She accepts and two and a half years later becomes the youngest person ever to circumnavigate. Co-written by Bernadette Brennan, the editor of *Cruising World* magazine.

VIDEOS

Around Cape Horn, A square-rigger rounding the tip of South America in some of the worst sea conditions you ever imagined. Narrated by crewmember Irving Johnson, the master of understatement.

The Last Sailors, narrated by Orson Welles. The story of primitive sailors who still today live off the sea in their primitive boats, from Brazil to Bangladesh to Indonesia.

Credit must be given to Ron Barr, owner of The Armchair Sailor Bookstore in Newport, R.I., for help in locating some of the older classics. The Armchair Sailor publishes a superb mail-order catalogue of sailing books and nautical paraphernalia, such as charts, binoculars, posters and weather instruments. Some of the books mentioned above can be purchased only from The Armchair Sailor. To order a catalog or find a book, write to The Armchair Sailor, 543 Thames St., Newport, R.I. 02840. Or call 1-800-29 CHART. □

25 OF THE WORLD'S BEST PLACES TO SAIL

By Lisa Gosselin, Senior Editor of Yachting *magazine.*

There is an old story about a tourist who stops at a farm in Maine to ask directions. The farmer puts his hand to his chin, thinks for a while, and then answers, "You can't get there from here."

Not being able to get there from here, at least by land, is usually what constitutes a great cruising area. In choosing the top 25 places in the world to sail, I looked for places—islands, craggy inlets, fjords, and so forth—where arriving by boat gives you an advantage. These are often places you can visit *only* by boat. In each case, either the geography or an undeveloped landscape makes staying aboard the obvious choice over traveling and sleeping on land.

Most of the places—in some cases a city, in some cases a country—have a history tied to the sea. Their locals look on people who come by boat as kindred spirits. Sail into St. Tropez and you will get a far friendlier reception than if you arrive in a Mercedes. Drop anchor in Tonga and you may be greeted by a native in a canoe.

For those without a boat of their own or the time to sail around the world, these ports don't have to be only distant dreams. Charter yachts—with or without captains— are available in each of the places mentioned, although in some areas, such as the Galápagos and Italy, it is illegal to "bareboat"—that is, charter a boat without a captain. Suggested charter companies are included in the Resources section for each cruise. Keep in mind, however, that several charter companies serve popular cruising areas such as the Caribbean and the Mediterranean.

Charter yachts usually have all of the necessary charts and guidebooks aboard. Make sure you have them before going on your own, however. The Armchair Sailor (543 Thames St., Newport, RI 02840, tel.: 800/292-4278) has a mail-order catalogue for charts and reading materials covering cruising grounds around the world.

UNITED STATES

Annapolis, Maryland

Annapolis is to the Chesapeake Bay what Newport is to New England. Old colonial homes line narrow streets that all seem to lead to the sea. Next to every deli is a yacht brokerage, and embroidered on just about every shirt pocket is the name of a yacht.

Home to the United States Naval Academy, Annapolis Harbor can field more maritime traffic on a Sunday afternoon than the Washington Beltway can cars. Submarines and motor cruisers share the Chesapeake Bay with more traditional craft like skipjacks and sailing canoes. But the bay also has many small coves and nooks to get away from it all.

The Chesapeake is an easy place for yachtsmen to become fat and lazy—fat on the catches of oysters and soft-shell crabs and lazy from rarely having to reef a sail. Winds are generally gentle—although they can be light and fluky in summer—and the seasons mild. In the event of a Chesapeake squall, there are many, many harbors to head into.

Resources
Information: Annapolis Tourism Office, 160 Duke of Glouces-ter St., Annapolis, MD 21401, tel.: 410/263-7940.
Charter operator: Annapolis Bay Charters, Box 4604, 7310 Edgewood Rd., Annapolis, MD 21403, tel.: 301/269-1776.
Charter bases: Annapolis, Havre de Grace, Oxford, Rock Hall.
Reading: A Cruising Guide to the Chesapeake, *by Stone, Blanchard, and Hays (New York: Putnam).*

The Florida Keys

I saw one of the most spectacular sunsets as I sailed into Key West for the first time. We had chartered a boat in Marathon and had sailed down the narrow, shallow channel on the Gulf side. Along the way, pelicans and a dolphin played in the bow wave. We anchored in the lee of a deserted mangrove island and waded in among the sand sharks and stone crabs. When we reached deeper, bluer water we could, on occasion, catch a silver glimmer of the fin of some great fish arcing through the air.

When we pulled into Key West, we saw a crowd assembled at the end of the pier. Jugglers and fire-eaters were performing, and the crowd itself could have been made up of circus performers. All were watching as the giant sun sank into a sea made mauve and turquoise where Atlantic and Gulf waters met.

The Keys are a great place to sail—winds are generally good and waters are teeming with marine life. At the John Pennekamp Reef State Park you can tie up to a buoy for some exceptional diving and snorkeling in this marine preserve. Little marinas dot both sides of the islands. You can sail in the Keys year-round. Winds tend to be fresh in the winter months, lighter in summer. Waters are generally easy to navigate, although things can be tricky around reefs.

Resources

Information: Florida Keys and Key West Visitors Bureau, Box 866, Key West, FL 33041, tel.: 305/296-3811 or 800/352-5397.

Charter operator: Treasure Harbor Charter Yachts, 200 Treasure

Harbor Dr., Islamorada, FL 33036, tel.: 305/852-2458 or 800/352-2628.

Charter bases: Miami, Key Largo, Islamorada.

Reading: A Cruising Guide to the Florida Keys, *by Frank Papy (Clearwater, FL: Cruising Guide Publications).*

Newport, Rhode Island

America's Cup racing left Newport in 1983, but this is still the greatest yachting center in North America. Vestiges of past America's Cups, the 134-foot J-Class yachts *Shamrock* and *Endeavour*, still sail in Narragansett Bay, their 17-story masts barely slipping under the Newport Bridge.

Onshore, the Museum of Yachting tracks the history of the sport, but in the harbor modern yachting history is made daily. Offshore racers take off around the world and statuesque Feadships—floating private compounds for a faceless few—command prime dock space downtown. Every weekend scores of boats ply the waters around Jamestown Island and anchor off the New York Yacht Club's summer residence, Harbor Court.

If you tire of the usual Newport summer bustle (and gridlocked streets), head east for the quiet harbors and gunk holes of Martha's Vineyard, Nantucket, or Block Island. On the islands you will find former whaling towns with pre-Revolutionary character, miles of empty beaches, and wind-swept moors.

The sailing season runs from June to October, with winds light in summer. Given the occasional strong currents and many rocks, navigating in and out of harbors can be tricky.

Resources

Information: Newport County Visitors Bureau, 23 America's Cup Ave., Newport, RI 02840, tel.: 401/849-8048 or 800/326-6030.

Charter operators: Bartram & Brakenhoff, 2 Marina Plaza, Goat Island, Newport, RI 02840, tel.: 401/846-7355; Dodson Boat Yard, Box 272, 194 Water St., Stonington, CT 06378, tel.: 203/535-1507.

Charter bases: Newport, RI; Stonington, CT; Yarmouthport, MA.

Reading: A Cruising Guide to the New England Coast, *by Duncan and Ware (New York: Putnam).*

Southwest Harbor, Maine

In Maine, where the coastline has more indents than a jigsaw puzzle, travel by boat is often easier than travel by land. Boats are the transport, the livelihood, and the soul of this part of the country. Lobster boats go out each day to pull in Maine's most prized catch.

From the Hinckley boatyard in Southwest Harbor on Mt. Desert Island, a handful of million-dollar yachts set out each year to meet new owners as far away as Europe, Australia, and Japan. Many of those owners return in their yachts—and with good reason: The cruising grounds beyond the two-inn town of Southwest Harbor are some of the finest in the world.

I can remember setting out up Somes Sound, just beyond Southwest Harbor, one day. The massive rounded top of Cadillac Mountain loomed ahead and hillsides fell steeply to form what is one of the only fjords on the East Coast. The cool gusts that heeled us over were rich with evergreen scents. Beyond the Sound, I could catch glimpses of little islands populated only by gulls and seals. There are two prices to pay, though, for this wild beauty: cold water and fog. Locals sometimes conquer the latter by using "potato navigation": throw a potato out and if it thuds, turn back; if it splashes, go ahead.

The sailing season runs from June to October, with generally steady breezes. However, fog, strong currents, and hidden rocks can make the sailing difficult.

Resources

Information: Bar Harbor Chamber of Commerce, Box BC, Cottage St., Bar Harbor, ME 04609, tel.: 207/288-3393; Acadia National Park, Box 177, Bar Harbor, ME 04609, tel.: 207/288-3338.

Charter operator: Hinckley Yacht Charters, Box 10, Bass Harbor, ME 04653, tel.: 207/244-5008

Charter bases: Bass Harbor, Boothbay Harbor, Camden, Falmouth, Rockland, Southwest Harbor.

Reading: A Cruising Guide to the Maine Coast, *by Hank and Jane Taft (Summit, PA: Tab Books).*

The North Channel

One of the most exhilarating sails I have had began from Chicago. The wind was blowing 30 and Lake Michigan had been whipped into a geography of waves unlike any I have seen in any ocean. It was a sunny day and we gleefully crashed through the steep crests, mouths open to the freshwater spray.

Unless you live on their shores, it is hard to imagine

the size and the power of the Great Lakes. The length of their coastline equals that of the entire East Coast. Unfortunately, along the white-sand beaches and the pine-rimmed shores, good, out-of-the-way anchorages are few and far between.

The 100-mile North Channel that separates Lakes Huron and Ontario has carved away a group of rocky islands. Among them is Manitoulin, the world's largest freshwater island. You can cruise into your own anchorages here, climb onto an island with no signs of habitation, and feel like you own the world.

A favorite among locals from Detroit to Duluth, the North Channel can get busy in the summer months. But there is always an island you can hide behind, and in September you can have the run of the place. Just be wary of sudden, violent storms and the many rocks and bars that make a good chart mandatory

Resources
Information: Ontario Travel, Queens Park, Toronto, ON M7A 2E5, tel.: 416/965-4008 or 800/668-2946.

Charter operator: Sailboats Inc., 250 Marina Dr., Superior, WI 54880, tel.: 800/472-7133.

Charter base: Gore Bay, Ontario.

Reading: Well-Favored Passage, *by Marjorie Cahn Brazer (Manchester, MI: Heron Books).*

Desolation Sound, Pacific Northwest

The coastline of the Inland Passage, from the popular San Juan Islands north of Seattle, up past Vancouver, Desolation Sound, and toward Alaska, offers some of the most spectacular scenery in North America. Hundred-foot waterfalls cascade down cliffs at the end of Princess Louisa inlet. You can sail right up to the edge of a glacier in Glacier Bay. All around are fir-covered islands and forests so thick the coastline is often inaccessible by land.

Standing on the rocky shore gathering mussels for dinner you may look up to find you are not alone. Ashore, bear and deer make this area their home and whales migrate up the deep dark waters to their feeding grounds each summer in Alaska.

Once past the San Juans, the winds can get light and fluky in the corridors formed by the high ridges of the islands. If you decide to head north, make sure you have plenty of fuel and provisions, because small towns and marinas are few and far between.

There are a few drawbacks: The sailing season is short—July through September—and summer winds tend to be light. Also, deep waters and strong currents can make anchoring difficult.

Resources
Information: San Juan Islands Tourism Cooperative, Box 65, Lopez, WA 98261, tel.: 206/468-3663; Southeast Alaska Tourism Council, Box 710, Juneau, AK 99802, tel.: 907/586-4777.

Charter operators: Desolation Sound Yacht Charters, 1797 Comox Ave., Suite 201, Comox, BC V9N 4A1, tel.: 604/339-7222; Fraser Charters, 3471 Via Lido, Newport Beach, CA 92663, tel.: 714/675-6960.

Charter bases: Anacortes, WA; Bellingham, WA; Seattle, WA; Vancouver, BC; Valdez, AK.

Reading: San Juan Islands Afloat and Afoot, *by Marge and Ted Mueller (Seattle: The Mountaineers).*

ASIA

Phuket, Thailand

In recent years, the waters off Phuket have become a last frontier for yachtsmen seeking perfect, out-of-the-way cruising grounds. Phuket's beaches are snow-white, its aquamarine waters bath-warm, and its marinas and hotels bits of Western culture in an Eastern landscape. Charter companies have made these waters more popular in recent years, but plenty of deserted anchorages are still here for the taking.

Beyond the swept-sand beaches and palms of Phuket lies the Andaman Sea and a variety of odd-shaped islands rising from it. Ko Phi Phi, the most famous, is shaped like a giant mushroom. Limestone cliffs rise above the sea, and occasionally you can see locals scaling them. Fishermen in broad-brimmed straw hats motor their dories and painted canoes in and out of the many sandy bays, and a lush green jungle grows almost to the edge of the sand.

The best sailing season is from November to April, when rain is sparse—unlike the monsoon season of summer and fall. There are plenty of protected coves with sandy bottoms for anchoring.

Resources

Information: Tourism Authority of Thailand, 5 World Trade Center, Suite 2449, New York, NY 10048, tel.: 212/432-0433.

Charter operator: Sunsail, 2 Prospect Park, 3347 N.W. 55th St., Ft. Lauderdale, FL 33309, tel.: 305/484-5246 or 800/327-2276.

Charter bases: Phuket, Krabi.

EUROPE

Isle of Wight, England

There might be prettier places off the English coast to sail, but none can match the sailing history of the Isle of Wight. At the mouth of a broad bay along England's southern coast, the waters around the island are where the first race in what would become the America's Cup series was held in 1851.

The Isle of Wight has remained a racing mecca, much along the lines of Newport and Annapolis in the United States. Events such as the Whitbread Round the World Race and the internationally contested Admiral's Cup start here. Perhaps *the* event of summer is Cowes Week, where hundreds of races for yachts of all sizes are held while the elder members of the exclusive Royal Yacht Squadron indulge in high tea ashore.

Cruising these waters provides a taste of all that is England, from the bustling industrial dockyard of Southampton to the quiet old town of Lymington. Shores are lined with castes and meadows and, farther west, high cliffs. Also characteristic of English cruising are the cold weather and occasionally strong tides.

Resources
Information: British Travel Centre, 12 Regent St., London SW1Y 4PQ, tel.: 44/071-730-3400; British Tourist Authority, 40 W. 57th St., New York, NY 10019, tel. 212/581–4700
Charter operator: Yachting Partners International, 28-29 Richmond Pl., Brighton, Sussex BN2 2NA, tel.: 44/273-571-720.
Charter bases: Southampton, Lymington.

Reading: South England Pilot, *by Robin Brandon (London: Imray/Huntingdon).*

The Canals, France

I have been a racing sailor my whole life, so the idea of lolling along an inland waterway motoring at four knots was not immediately appealing. However, my first trip down the Canal du Midi from Toulouse to Carcassone changed my mind. Although it took time to get used to drifting at a pace at which donkeys pass you, I came to love traveling down the winding canals that delve into France's quiet countryside. The smell of lavender and thyme growing wild along the shores of the Canal du Midi will forever haunt my memory.

On a canal outside of Paris, I met a lock-keeper who took us in to show us medals he had earned in World War II. In Burgundy, vintners insisted we sample their wines. Short bikes ride from nearly every canal led to castles and fortified villages well off the beaten tourist paths.

The best season is April through November, and the biggest navigational challenge is getting through the locks. Otherwise, you simply follow the canal.

Resources

Information: France-Anjou Navigation, Quai National, 72300 Sablé-sur-Sarthe, France; Bourgogne Voies Navigables, 1 quai de la République, 8900 Auxerre, France; French Government Tourist Office, 610 Fifth Ave., New York, NY 10020, tel.: 900/990-0040.

Charter operator: Blake's Vacations, 4918 Dempster St., Skokie, IL 60077, tel.: 708/982-0561.

Charter bases: Toulouse, Sète, Paris.

Reading: Inland Waterways of France, *by E.E. Benest (London: Imray/Huntingdon).*

The Côte d'Azur, France

If you reserve dock spaces well in advance, the best way to see the Côte d'Azur is undoubtedly by yacht. From the old-fashioned fishing port of St. Tropez to the new marinas below the high rises of Monaco, this stretch of coastline offers breathtaking views, world-famous museums, and all the muscular nightlife one expects of the Riveria. From the water you can see long boardwalks with ornate buildings, and towering cliffs adorned with private villas and palaces. Inland are the snow-capped maritime Alps.

In the summer months, travel by land means battling traffic jams. Unfortunately, the situation in marinas is often not much better, and the docking scene is frequently crowded. October is the ideal time—also the time of year when the famous Nioulargue races start in St. Tropez. The old town is jammed from quay to quay with sailing yachts—giant classics to modern maxis. Festivals and dancing go on all night in the streets and nightclubs. Although you can sail from May to November, breezes pick up in October, when the summer vacation crowds are gone and you can leisurely pick your way down the coast.

Resources
Information: Comité Régional du Tourisme de Riviera-Côte-d'Azur, 55 Promenade des Anglais, 0600 Nice, France; French Government Tourist Office, 610 Fifth Ave., New York, NY 10020, tel.: 900/990-0400.

Charter operator: Yachting Plus, c/o Le Boat, Inc., Box E, Maywood, NJ 07607, tel.: 201/342-1838 or 800/922-0291.

Charter bases: St. Tropez, Monaco, San Remo.
Reading: South France Pilot, by Robin Brandon (London: Imray/Huntingdon).

The Greek Islands, Greece

Look hard enough in these fabled cruising grounds and you can recognize, if not Odysseus's landfalls, then certainly the historic landmarks: the Minoan ruins on Crete, the ancient amphitheater on Delos, Santorini—once thought to be the origin of the myth of Atlantis.

From the olive groves on Corfu to the pillars of Rhodes near the Turkish coast, thousands of islands dot the waters of the Ionian, Aegean, and Mediterranean seas. On nearly each, ancient ruins and whitewashed towns loom up above the sapphire waters. You could spend a lifetime cruising here and not retrace your steps.

The obstacles to making this a true cruising paradise are the distances between islands, the scarcity of good harbors, and the high winds—known as the meltemi—that can whip the seas into a fury only Zeus might be able to handle. The best sailing is in spring and autumn; in summer the meltemi blow hot and strong. Holding grounds must be sought out.

Resources
Information: Greek National Tourist Organization, Olympic Tower, 5th floor, 645 Fifth Ave., New York, NY 10022, tel.: 212/421-5777.
Charter operator: GPSC Charters, Ltd., 600 St. Andrews Rd., Philadelphia, PA 19118, tel.: 215/247-3903 or 800/732-7686.
Charter bases: Poros, Corfu, Rhodes, Piraeus.

Reading: Greek Waters Pilot, *by Rod Heikell (London: Imray/Huntingdon).*

Sardinia, Italy

The Kubla Khan might have had Xanadu, but the Aga Khan got Sardinia, the rocky island off Italy's Tuscan coast where he and a consortium have built a pleasure dome, known as Porto Cervo, for yachtsmen. Porto Cervo is renowned as one of the most elite ports in the world, and dock fees can run to $1,000 per night; count on spending double that each day if you spend any time and money ashore. From here, some of Europe's most elegant yachts head out to the few beaches that meet the azure sea.

For a taste of old Sardinia, head north. Here the wild beauty of the island is apparent in great jumbles of rocks that pour straight down into the crystal depths and the wildflowers that cling to the cliffsides.

It is less than a day's sail to the Tuscan coast from Sardinia. In the little ports of Porto Ercole on Monte Argentario, boat-builders still practice their time-honored trade. To the north, Portofino's villas cascade down hillsides; to the south, Capri has a magical feel. The best sailing is from May to November, when the winds are light and warm. Beware of the stong, northwesterly maestrale winds.

Resources
Information: Italian Government Travel Office, 630 Fifth Ave., Suite 1565, New York, NY 10111, tel.: 212/245-4822.
Charter operator: Sunsail, 2 Prospect Park, 3347 N.W. 55th St., Ft. Lauderdale, FL 33309, tel.: 800/327-2276.
Charter bases: Portofino, Elba, Capri.

Reading: Italian Waters Pilot, *by Rod Heikell (London: Imray/Huntingdon).*

Bodrum to Marmaris, Turkey

Most sailing adventures seem to take you far away from civilization; vacations on land often take you to the heart of it. Cruising Turkey's southern coast combines both. Marmaris, once home to the armada of an Ottoman sultan, now serves as home port for a large fleet of modern charter yachts as well as the traditional Turkish gulets. Byzantine ruins cap the hilltops that loom high above the deep, clear waters. At Kekova you can snorkel over the remains of ancient buildings and sarcophagi. In Sedir Adalari, you can cruise to the beach where, legend has it, Cleopatra ordered tons of sand to be shipped in to create a hideaway for herself and Marc Antony.

Between the occasional tourist resorts are small fishing villages where you can tie your stern to the quays and barter at the local markets for fresh fish, rugs, and local crafts. Steep hills, pine groves, and rocky beaches are the principal features of the scenery in between.

Many yachtsmen prefer the quiet waters of the Gulf of Gokova and its many islands to the windswept seas surrounding the Greek archipelago. The strong meltemi winds can also blow in Turkey (primarily in the summer), but they are not as fierce, and Turkish waters tend to be more protected. The sailing season runs from April to November.

Resources
Information: Turkish Culture and Information Office, 821 UN

Plaza, New York, NY 10017, tel.: 212/687-2194.
Charter operator: GPSC Charters, Ltd., 600 St. Andrews Rd.,
Philadelphia, PA 19118, tel.: 215/247-3903 or 800/732-6786.
Charter bases: Bodrum, Marmaris.
Reading: Turkish Waters Pilot, by Rod Heikell (London: Imray/Huntingdon).

Dalmation Coast, Yugoslavia

From Brioni, the northern island where Tito built his vacation home, to the Venetian-style city of Dubrovnik several hundred miles south, each of the once-quiet little islands and ports that line the Dalmation coast offers something special; let's hope the current political maelstrom quiets down so visitors can drop anchor again. For example, much of a medieval town still stands on the island of Korcula, reputed to be Marco Polo's birthplace. A short overland hike on Mljet leads to a large lake, and via ferry you can reach a 12th-century Benedictine monastery that sits in its center.

Although some of the islands have become tourist resorts—often nudist tourist resorts—the vineyards that grow on the terraced hillsides and the calamari and other catch that fishermen bring home still provide much of the sustenance and livelihood for local people.

With the exception of the occasionally fierce bora, winds are light to moderate. The water is warm, and there are enough tiny harbors, with good holding ground for anchoring, to allow you to have an island to yourself. The sailing season is April through November; in winter the bora can blow up to 50 knots.

Resources

Information: Yugoslav National Tourist Office, 630 Fifth Ave., New York, NY 10111, tel.: 212/757-2801.

Charter operators: Sunsail, 2 Prospect Park, 3347 N.W. 55th St., Ft. Lauderdale, FL 33309, tel.: 305/484-5246 or 800/327-2276; The Moorings, 19354 U.S. 19N, Suite 402, Clearwater, FL 34624, tel.: 813/535-1446 or 800/535-7289.

Charter bases: Dubrovnik, Split.

Reading: Adriatic Pilot, by T. Thompson and D. Thompson (London: Imray/Huntingdon).

MEXICO AND THE CARIBBEAN

The Abacos, Bahamas

The clearest waters in the world, I am told, can be found
in the Bahamas. Sailors who have watched the flukes of an
anchor dig into the sand 40 feet below know this. In fact,
the Bahamas have lent their name to a navigational style
called "Bahamian navigation" that, even in the age of radar
and Loran, is still used. Its basic tenets: Stand on the bow
on a bright day around noon and look down. Often, because
of the unmarked shifting sandbars and reefs, this is the only
safe method of making your way through the islands.

Until recently, there have been few facilities for yachts
in the Bahamas, and restrictions on chartering have made
access difficult. Now areas like Eleuthera and Marsh Harbor in the Abacos are quickly developing into cruise and
charter ports. As they do, more and more people are finding their way to the white beaches that dot many of the
2,400 low-lying cays and exploring the old colonies on
islands that are still privately owned.

Good 20-knot breezes last throughout the winter, and
hurricane season stretches from July to November. A few
cautionary notes: Don't trust the charts, because the reefs
and bars move quickly, and watch for strong currents and
riptides.

Resources
*Information: Bahamas Tourist Office, 150 E. 52nd St., New
York, NY 10022, tel.: 212/758-02777 or 800/627-7281.*
*Charter operator: Sunsail, 2 Prospect Park, 3347 N.W. 55th
St., Ft. Lauderdale, FL 33309, tel.: 305/484-5246 or*

800/327-2276.
Charter bases: Marsh Harbor, Hope Town, Eleuthera.
Reading: Yachtsman's Guide to the Bahamas *(North Miami, FL: Tropic Isle Publishers).*

British and U.S. Virgin Islands

When you come to the Virgin Islands, you have arrived in yachting heaven: perhaps the world's premier cruising arena. The Virgin Islands are home to the largest fleet of charter yachts in the world—more than 500 yachts in all.

The 100 or so mountainous islands that make up this chain feature crescents of white-sand beaches, palm-topped sandbars, rocky slopes, and turquoise waters. Below the surface are all the colors and activity of an aquarium. Nearly every island has its driftwood beach bar—Foxy's on Jost Van Dyke is my favorite; you can order lobster at noon and feast on it at dinner, washing it down with a piña colada. Each island is no more than a few hours by boat from another—a quick jaunt through the flat waters between islands. That means many options to fill up the sailing day, the sail around St. John's being one of my favorites.

Cruising in the Virgins has many logistical advantages. You can sail year-round, and breezes are generally fresh, reaching the 20-knot range around Christmas. Waters are usually calm, bottoms sandy, navigation easy, and reefs visible.

Resources
Information: British Virgin Islands Tourist Board, 370 Lexington Ave., Suite 511, New York, NY 10017, tel.: 212/696-0400 or 800/835-8530; U.S. Virgin Islands Government Tourist Office, 1270 Ave. of the Americas, New York, NY 10020, tel.: 212/582-4521.

Charter operator: The Moorings, 19354 U.S. 19N, Suite 402, Clearwater, FL 34624, tel.: 813/535-1446 or 800/535-7289.

Charter bases: St. Thomas and St. John, U.S.Virgin Islands; Tortola and Virgin Gorda, British Virgin Islands.

Reading: A Cruising Guide to the Eastern Caribbean, *by Donald Street (New York: Norton).*

Antigua, Leeward Islands

Traveling between the large islands of St. Martin and Antigua can mean rolling ocean conditions and long sails. So unless you have a few weeks, it's best to explore the little islands and bays that surround the two islands. Although St. Martin has fresh baguettes and Yves St. Laurent boutiques, and St. Barts is a gem of an old French fishing port, Antigua tugs at my heart. Around English and Falmouth harbors goats graze on the hillside, and the roads are largely unpaved. In these large harbors Lord Nelson claimed and fortified are some of the world's most beautiful yachts. Hundred-foot classics tie up to the stone bollards in front of a handful of the well-preserved stone buildings that populate the Dockyard.

One of the best ways to see Antigua is by signing up for Sailing Week. This regatta, held at the end of April, draws an international caliber of race boats, scores of old classics, and plenty of just-plain cruisers for a week of easy racing from beach to beach. Sailing days are followed by nightly parties, spiced by rum, bikini contests, and the beat of steel drums.

Resources

Information: Antigua and Barbuda Department of Tourism, Thames and Long Sts., St. John's, Antigua, tel.: 809/462-3702.

Charter operator: Nicholson Yacht Charters, 432 Columbia St., Cambridge, MA 02141, tel.: 617/225-0555 or 800/662-6066.

Charter bases: St. Martin, Antigua.

Reading: A Cruising Guide to the Leeward Islands, *by Chris Doyle (Clearwater, FL: Cruising Guide Publications).*

The Grenadines, Windward Islands

Beyond the Caribbean world of beach bars and resort hotels are the Windward Islands. South of Martinique, the Caribbean seems to function with fewer tourists. In the inner rain forests of St. Vincent, women still haul the banana harvest in huge baskets balanced on their heads. Markets are infused with the scent of nutmeg and other spices, and the hills and beaches are dotted with the tiny, brightly painted homes of fishermen whose nets dry in the front yard.

Although there are few facilities for yachtsmen and provisions can be difficult to come by, these islands are a superb sailing ground. Among my favorite stops along the way is Bequia—where a tiny boatyard on the beach has crafted lovely cruising boats for the likes of singer/songwriter Bob Dylan. A short sail away from Bequia's quiet little port is Mustique, where, if you sit in Basil's Bar long enough, you might spot Mick Jagger.

The most spectacular anchorage—I'd risk to say in the entire Caribbean—is south in the Tobago Keys. A handful of tiny, sand-rimmed islands form a bay that is protected by concentric reefs. The water is a spectrum of greens, blues, and purples. Fishermen pull up and offer to catch grouper or lobster for your dinner, and a cool breeze keeps the halyards clanking. Expect breezes in the 20s and large ocean swells between islands.

Resources

Information: French West Indies Tourist Board, c/o French Government Tourist Office, 610 Fifth Ave., New York, NY 10020, tel.: 900/990-0400; St. Vincent and the Grenadines Tourist Office, 801 2nd Ave., 21st floor, New York, NY 10017, tel.: 212/687-4981 or 800/729-1726.

Charter operator: The Moorings, 18354 U.S. 19N, Suite 402, Clearwater, FL 34624, tel.: 813/535-1446 or 800/535-7289.

Charter bases: St. Lucia, St. Vincent, Martinique, Grenada.

Reading: Exploring the Windward Islands, *by Chris Doyle (Clearwater, FL: Cruising Guide Publications).*

Sea of Cortés, Mexico

Only a few dedicated fishermen know all of the secrets of the Sea of Cortés, although yachtsmen are quickly learning a few of them. This body of water between mainland Mexico and the Baja peninsula is home to the most concentrated population of marine life in the world—perhaps because so few boats and people have discovered it.

Anchor alone off the desolate rocky shores of Baja and the only sounds you will hear are echoes of your own voice off the worn ochre boulders ashore. Or you might hear the splash of a seal as it wriggles into the glassy water or the crash of a whale's fluke. Few people I have known who have sailed here have come back without a tale of some encounter with marine wildlife.

The sea life makes up for nonexistent nightlife and few

facilities for yachts. A few resorts have sprung up, and charter bases such as The Moorings in Puerto Escondido offer good starting points. If you are planning to sail here on your own, provision well before going and bring fishing line and bait. The sailing season runs from October to May, with better winds during the winter months.

Resources

Information: Mexican Government Tourism Office, 405 Park Ave., New York, NY 10022, tel.: 212/755-7261.

Charter operator: The Moorings, 1305 U.S. 19N, Suite 402, Clearwater, FL 34624, tel.: 813/535-1446 or 800/535-7289.

Charter bases: Puerto Escondido, Cabo San Lucas, Ensenada.

Reading: Charlie's Charts: Western Coast of Mexico, *by Charles Wood (Surrey, BC).*

SOUTH AMERICA

Cape Horn

Infamous as the "eater of ships and men," Cape Horn remains the greatest challenge a sailor can face. Winds gust regularly to 60 knots and 30-foot waves roil waters sprinkled with iceberg bits around South America's southern tip. In the years before the Panama Canal, sailors dreaded this passage, and rounding the Horn today is still a mark of distinction.

Conditions aren't always man-eating. When, on a magazine assignment a few years ago, Fraser Heston (Charlton's son) cruised around the Horn with three friends, he wrote about pleasant 20- to 30-knot winds and about feasting on riverbed mussels and fresh local lamb. Nevertheless, this end of the earth is for the hardy few—mainly circumnavigating racers and the occasional yacht pausing before setting off across Drake's Passage to the Antarctic.

Areas not far from the Horn itself are more hospitable to cruising. North, along the Strait of Magellan and the Tierra del Fuego archipelago, are some of the most awe-inspiring landscapes on the planet. The glacier-covered Andes plunge down into the straits. Lush woods grow in the low-lying islands and ice-blue water cascades from the high peaks. But the cruising is not easy. Deep waters and williwaw winds that gust down from the Andes make special anchoring techniques necessary.

Resources

Information: Chile Consulate General, 510 W. Sixth St., Suite 1204, Los Angeles, CA 90014, tel.: 213/624-6357.

Charter operator: Ocean Voyages, 1709 Bridgeway, Sausalito, CA 94965, tel.: 415/332-4681.

Charter bases: Punta Arenas, Chile; Ushuaia, Argentina.

Reading: Two Against Cape Horn, *by Hal Roth (New York: Norton).*

Galápagos Islands

Getting to the Galápagos, 600 miles off the coast of Ecuador, is no easy matter. But the trip is well worth it: The 13 islands are a last refuge for species that have evolved in isolation from the rest of the planet. The Galápagos' arid volcanic landscape has not changed much since Charles Darwin visited and wrote of his findings in *The Origin of the Species.*

The government keeps a tight reign on visitor entry, and tortoises still outnumber humans by more than two to one. Private yachts are restricted to certain sailing areas unless they receive special permits and are guided by a naturalist. Only a handful of anchorages are open to private yachts.

So the best way to see these islands and the blue-footed boobies, giant tortoises, and iguanas is aboard a small charter yacht. Charter captains know of the most scenic sails along the rocky coasts and their (naturalist) guides fill you in on the flora and fauna as you sail. A package-style land and sea tour is another way to explore the Galápagos, but a chartered cruise is by far the more enjoyable way to go.

Resources

Information: Galápagos Islands Tourism Information, 18 E. 41st St., New York, NY 10017, tel.: 212/545-0711 or 800/872-4256.

Charter operators: Ocean Voyages, 1709 Bridgeway, Sausalito, CA 94965, tel.: 415/332-4681; Tumbaco Inc., Box 1036, Isles Professional Center, Suite 11, Punta Gorda, FL 33951, tel.: 813/637-4660 or 800/247-2925.

Charter base: San Cristóbal.

Reading: Voyage of the Beagle, *by Charles Darwin (New York: Doubleday).*

SOUTH PACIFIC

Bay of Islands, New Zealand

Sailing is to a New Zealander what football is to an American. The entire country has rallied around the recent America's Cup challenges led by New Zealand banker Sir Michael Fay, who caused a great stir in 1988 when he challenged the San Diego Yacht Club for the America's Cup. His home club was the tiny Mercury Bay Boating Club, the clubhouse of which is a car on Mercury Bay's white beach.

Sailing is not only one of the best ways to explore the two islands that make up this spectacular country it is one of the only ways. This is a small country and much of it remains undeveloped. The fury and force of nature dominate the land and the waterways: Auckland is built on 16 extinct volcanoes, inland geysers spout steam and spray, and massive glaciers have carved out the peaks of the South Island.

The most popular cruising ground is in the North Island's Bay of Islands, where the weather is mild almost year-round. Grassy meadows where sheep graze and wooded hills look as if they could have been pulled from an English landscape. Hundreds of little islands and bays, with hospitable villages and excellent little marinas, dot this area north of Auckland.

The best time to sail is from October to June, when winds are steady and the weather mild. Deep, clear waters and well-marked charts make navigation relatively easy.

Resources

Information: New Zealand Tourist Office, Suite 1530, 10960 Wilshire Blvd., Los Angeles, CA 90024, tel.: 213/477-8241.

Charter operator: Rainbow Yacht Charters, 3471 Via Lido, Suite 206, Newport Beach, CA 92663, tel.: 800/634–8820.

Charter bases: Auckland, Whangarei.

Reading: New Zealand's Bay of Islands, *by Claire Jones (Opua, NZ: Port of Opua Trading Co.).*

Bora Bora, French Polynesia

Bora Bora is a favorite anchorage among experienced yachtsmen, but it is only one of French Polynesia's Society Islands, all of which can cast a spell over sailors. Over the lagoon in Bora Bora rise two extinct volcanoes whose tops snare wispy clouds. The bay is lined with palms and its waters colored green by reefs. The inland jungle is the garden of fruits and flowers that inspired the myth of Bali Hai in *South Pacific*.

Bora Bora stands out among islands in this group, many of which have succumbed to various degrees of commercialization. Tahiti is a small metropolis—but a good place to get spare parts, provisions, or anything else you might need if you're on your way around the world. Huahine, one of the smaller islands, still remains much as it was a century ago with lots of farmland and few paved roads.

May to October is the best time to sail, because cyclones are a possibility at other times of year. Coral reefs and strong surf around nearly every harbor entrance can make entry difficult.

Resources

Information: French Government Tourist Office, 610 Fifth Ave., New York, NY 10020, tel.: 900/990-0400.

Charter operator: The Moorings, 1305 U.S. 19N, Suite 402, Clearwater, FL 34624, tel.: 813/535-1446 or 800/535-7289.

Charter bases: Raiatéa, Papeete.

Reading: Cruising Guide to Tahiti and the Society Islands, *by Marcia Davock (Clearwater, FL: Cruising Guide Publications).*

Tonga

Almost on the international date line lies the Kingdom of Tonga, a port of call for most circumnavigators. Unlike the Polynesian group, which is made up of distinct islands that can be a half-day's sail away, the 160 islets in four groups that make up the Kingdom of Tonga are strung together in chains of limestone outcroppings, coral reefs, and sandy atolls. The interiors hide active volcanoes and waterfalls, ancient tombs, and eerie caverns. Away from the main island of Vavau, the people live off their tiny plots of land and spend their days farming, weaving, or making the tapa cloth the islands are known for. King Taufa'ahau Tupou IV still rules this island kingdom, and canoe races and pig roasts are important parts of every major celebration. Cannibalism, once rampant, was wiped out hundreds of years ago, although Captain Bligh's party was reluctant to set foot ashore on these islands after being cast adrift from the *Bounty* in 1789.

The best sailing is May to October, with typhoon season running from December to March. Strong currents can rip around the islands, but good anchorages can be found within the lagoons.

Resources

Information: General Consulate Kingdom of Tonga, 360 Post St., Suite 604, San Francisco, CA 94108, tel.: 415/781–0365; Pacific Area Travel Association, 1 Montgomery St., West Tower Suite 1750, San Francisco, CA 94108, tel.: 415/986–4646.

Charter operator: The Moorings, 1305 U.S. 19N, Suite 402, Clearwater, FL 34624, tel.: 813/535–1446 or 800/535–7289.

Charter bases: Vavau, Nukualofa.

Reading: Cruising Guide to the Kingdom of Tonga *(Clearwater, FL: Cruising Guide Publications).*

The Whitsunday Islands, Australia

On Whitsunday in the late 1770s, Captain James Cook sailed into the tropical islands off the north coast of Australia. Since then, the islands, now known as the Whitsundays, have become one of the most popular cruising grounds south of the Caribbean. More than 100 islands—the tops of a sunken mountain range—rise out of the turquoise sea. Rocky and covered with a low-lying scrub of pines and eucalyptus, the islands fall away to coral reefs below the water's surface. On most of the islands you can find sandy bays and beaches that offer perfect overnight anchorages.

Nearly every sailing Aussie on vacation seems to head for the Whitsundays. Still, beyond the famous resort islands like Hayman Island and Shute Harbor lie the undeveloped areas that form the Great Barrier Reef Marine Park.

Snorkel along the reefs off Hook Island or watch the swarms of butterflies flitting by the creek at Butterfly Bay. Climb the hills above Nara Inlet to see the caves with aborigine paintings—some dating back 8,000 years. The islands are close together, so it's easy to do all of this in a week.

The sailing season runs from April to October. Light trade winds make for pleasant sailing, but strong currents demand that you check your anchor frequently.

Resources

Information: Australian Tourist Commission, 2121 Ave. of the Stars, Suite 1200, Los Angeles, CA 90067, tel.: 213/552-1988.

Charter operators: Hamilton Island Charters, Box 35, Hamilton Island 4803, Australia, tel.: 079/46-9999.

Charter bases: Hamilton Island, Shute Harbor, Pioneer Bay.

Reading: Fatal Shore, *by Robert Hughes (New York: Knopf).*

About the Author

Michael B. McPhee spent fifteen years as a wire
service and newspaper reporter, before turning to
magazine editing and free-lance writing. His work has
appeared in many major newspapers, including *The
New York Times*, *The Washington Post*, and *The Boston
Globe*, as well as *The International Herald Tribune*.

Since learning to sail while in college, he has
logged more than 10,000 miles of off-shore passages.
He has owned a number of boats, ranging from a
Hobie Cat to a wooden Norwegian 8-Meter sloop.

Born in Aspen, Colorado, he graduated from the
University of Colorado and was decorated twice for
combat in Vietnam. He divides his time between
Boston and San Francisco.